Gretchen Harvey
15 October
1988
WHC-Wichita

Native American Women

Native American Women

A CONTEXTUAL BIBLIOGRAPHY

Rayna Green

Indiana University Press   Bloomington

This book was produced from magnetic tape provided by the author.

Manufactured in the United States of America

Library of Congress Cataloging in Publication Data

Green, Rayna.
Native American women.

Includes index.
1. Indians of North America—Women—Bibliography.
2. Eskimos—Women—Bibliography. 3. Aleuts—Women—
Bibliography. I. Title.
Z1209.2.N67G75   1983   [E98.W8]   016.3054'8897   82-48571
ISBN 0-253-33976-6   2   3   4   5   87   86

Contents

Preface

NOTE: References in the Preface and Introduction are keyed to the numbered bibliographic entries. Citations are not meant to be inclusive on any topic, merely exemplary, and the index can further fill out citations.

The bibliography herein represents three years of work for me, some of it sporadic, some of it intense, and 200 years of writing for many. Several before me have made efforts at bibliographic compilation, and many have helped me in this effort—male and female, Indian and non-Indian. I am grateful to Terrie Duda, Roger Long, Clara Sue Kidwell, Shirley Hill Witt, and my students at Dartmouth College, Helene Quick, Michael Green, and many others who shared citations with me and assisted in the production of various versions of this bibliography. To Owanah Anderson, Kim Rankin, Sedelta Verble, Noalene Clanton, and Fran Walton of the Ohoyo Resource Center, I am thankful for the support and encouragement in producing the first offprint edition of this work, one that was distributed to Native people involved in educational development for Indians (232). I will remain grateful to Emily Fayen, of Dartmouth College Baker Library, for her development of the fine computer program and invaluable, patient assistance in the production of the computerized bibliography and index. And to a former editor of *Signs: Journal Of Women in Culture and Society,* Joan Burstyn, I owe thanks for her encouragement of my first review of the literature on a major scale (233). Finally, my deepest thanks goes to the staff and officers of the Muskiwinni Foundation for their generous support of this work. While I owe much to many, any errors, deficiencies, and omissions in the work are mine alone, and I bear sole responsibility for them. However, since the entries rest in a computer memory bank, I can update the work at any time. For that update, I will again rely on the kindness and interest of scholars and colleagues who will share their knowledge with me. I look forward to that relationship and to the use that many may make of this work.

Because I wanted to make this bibliography useful to the widest range of people, I have included entries from the widest range of materials and approaches. I have tried through the introduction, and the index and annotations, to interpret the material, to direct the reader for a richer, more varied use. What is here concerns Native North American women, including Alaskan and Canadian. I have excluded references to South American and U.S. Chicana women, except to point to decent bibliographies. References are to the United States unless otherwise noted. I have cited materials on Native women's art, writing, traditional crafts, and cuisine, only when the focus of the work was on the women who cooked, wrote, painted, potted, or when the focus was on those forms of work as "women's" work per se. In order to avoid needless repetition of material in other bibliographies, I have excluded material which is contained in standard ethnographies or histories. What resides herein is specifically about Native women as members of groups or as individuals. Readers should consult the ethnographic atlases, tribal bibliographies, and standard culture area or tribal ethnographies and histories for references to specific topics (e.g. menstrual taboos) or general areas of interest (e.g. child-rearing). I have included citations for works on these topics only when particular works focused on femaleness, and on women in general or particular, rather than on the rite, the custom, the ceremony, and so forth. Unfortunately, while looking, readers will never find much material on Native women, they will find piecemeal but useful references that can be factored in with other works and thus fill in parts of old puzzles or create new ones. I have not included unpublished conference recordings and other audio-visual treatments of Native women, all to be found through inter-library loan, microprint editions, audio-visual offices in educational institutions and recording company catalogs. Some obscure items can be examined at the Library of Congress or secured through interlibrary loan, while others, some Canadian reports for example, must be got directly from the source of the original work. But most general items are easily accessible to readers with access to a university or decent public library.

The works listed here are a tribute to the interest many writers, scholarly and popular, have taken in Native women, and increasingly, to the attention Native women pay to themselves. Because I realized that many readers would find writings by Native people of inherent interest, I have included tribal designations, next to the names of authors, where such a designation could be determined. It is to these sister scholars and writers, and to those women and men who pay honor to the truth about Native women in their writing that I dedicate and offer this book.

Introduction

In a recent review essay on anthropological writing about women, Rayna Rapp noted the "coming of age of the anthropology of women" by citing the enormous production of material in the late seventies (515). After examining more than 700 bibliographic items on Native North American women dating from the late seventeenth century, over two-thirds of which were produced in the twenty years between 1960 and 1980, I can say that the study of Native women is flowering. But, with Rapp, I can also say that a "fully developed body of literature looms in the distance." There have been trends, thematic and methodological consistencies, even topical passions in scholarly and popular writing about Native North American women; in fact, those trends and passions constitute a major problem for scholars and Native Americans alike. But, as with all women's studies, things are changing for the better. New trends, new forms of change, new kinds of people working in the field—all make an optimism about the future possible even while old ideas and old styles of scholarship persist.

My review of the literature, here treated chronologically, has left me with the conviction that Native women have been neither neglected nor forgotten. They have captured hearts and minds, but, as studies of other women have demonstrated, the level and substance of most passion for them has been selective, stereotyped, and damaging. From John Smith's initial creation of New World nobility in Princess Pocahontas (574) down to my own and other Native women's formal repudiations of his "Myth America," Native women have been studied to death or to distraction (114,226,235,436). Most of the clichés seem to be irresistible. Yet, somewhere between Smith's ploy of creating dead princesses and saints (Kateri Tekakwitha) in order to make live white male heroes and General Sheridan's preference for murdering "squaws" and their children ("nits make lice," said he at Sand Creek), there has been a middle scholarly road.

Given American scholars' almost pathological attachment to Indian wars, horsemen of the Plains and "End of the Trail" chiefs, I suppose we should be grateful that anything at all has been written about Native women.

1

Yet, anthropologists, historians, government agents and novelists alike came to be as intellectually enamoured of Native women as trappers, priests, playwrights, and soldiers were sexually smitten. The new mythology, born on remote reservations where Indian people were removed in the last century, included women on the list of endangered but not tamed species living in those preserves. Memorialized on stamps and coins like those other threatened creatures, the buffalo, Native women and men came to be the property (and the reservation, the laboratory) of scholars who measured, tested and speculated on them. However, scholars' passions were reserved for the old and dying parts of Native culture, just as land-hungry settlers' passions were for dead and dying Indians. But live and grow in number Native people did, and urban, nonreservation, culturally changed Indians later kept generations of social workers, educators, and psychologists well employed in the twentieth century. For years, studies of cultural dissolution (called change and acculturation studies) predicted Indian demise, though now and again some fleeting positive portrait of living traditions and healthy peoples was produced. The compelling figure for scholars remained the alcoholic, suicidal, tragic male and his most recent surrogate, the American landscape.

The some 200 years of occasional and desultory writing on Native women before 1900 produced little specifically about Native women, though the specific references to Pocahontas set the tone for the next two centuries of writing, and virtually created a cottage industry in Pocahontas plays, novels, biographies and critical literature (17,44-45,74,92,201,235,262, 293,314,450,527,671). Non-Indians generally ignored work by Native men and women, virtually entirely in favor of the mythologizing found in diaries, missionary accounts, travel tales and popular folklore (songs, stories, etc.), and the mythology grew without reference to those accounts which eschewed mythology. For example, two early novels by Native men, Boudinot and Pokagon, had virtually no audience, even though they were heavily influenced in attitude (toward women and other matters) and style by European writing (72,508). Unlike Native American men, Native women were elusive for those who did not have personal relationships with them, while relationships with unbiased observers were few. For those trappers, "squaw men," and missionaries who did write about Native women, truth neither served their best interests nor was available. Distant princesses and saints were acceptable, but frequently matriarchal, matrifocal and matrilineal societies were neither acceptable nor comprehensible to members of the European patriarchies, who misunderstood Eastern tribes so profoundly that they sabotaged their own treaties regularly in making them with men who did not have the right to make such decisions. Few early Native women wrote their own words down (21), and writers who chose to record notes about early figures usually had their own religious, political agendas at heart in telling of women like Kateri Tekakwitha, the "saint of the Mohawks" (110,113,626). Even when Winnemucca and the LaFlesche sisters, Suzette and Suzanne, became well-known activists and lecturers, and in Winnemucca's case, a writer, reformist women and men gave them a voice to further their own causes—often ones that had little relevance to Indian causes (33,288,425,493-94,526,655). Even those non-Indian works sympathetic to Indian causes and Indian women, like Helen Hunt Jackson's famous reformist novel, *Ramona,* played on an image of Native women that was as sentimental and stereotyped as any penny dreadful could be (306). Most Native women of power and of note either to their own people or to whites, Sarah Winnemucca, the LaFlesches, Molly Brant, Nancy Ward, Mary Musgrove, or Madame Montour, received little attention until the twentieth century (343). When scholars finally took an interest, they limited the terms of that interest. For example, they discovered matriarchy among the Iroquois, spending sixty years in debates about that one instance, while other versions of matriarchy went unstudied, eventually disappearing or changing dramatically in the meantime (53,107,117). Debates over Pocahontas', Sacajawea's, and Tekakwithas' historicity remained the historians preoccupation, while a vast procession of significant tribal leaders passed by unnoticed or with bare nods. In these decades too, with the exception of early mild interest in traditional taletelling and language which persisted for three centuries (307,322,340,479-80,538-39,578-79), the initial forms of interest in women's "culture"—art, maternal behavior, religion—were often no more than shallow inquiries into "rites" and "customs" (239-40,284,406,413).

The three decades before 1930 introduced new topics—the discovery of the Southwest, for example, and of individual figures. Students of Plains, Northwest Coast, and Inuit life discovered women (98,219,355,400,488-90) and a few "custom" studies (menstrual, marital, and ceremonial) appeared, later to dominate the literature for years (365,495,618). The period also brought some historians to a "discovery" of Sacajawea and the

LaFlesche sisters, those interested in culture and politics to a further recognizance of the importance of the Iroquoian matriarchies (138,221, 541,639), and others to a beginning interest in social welfare (6,525). And the first two decades brought more words from Native women—from the educated, upper-class Cherokee leader, Narcissa Owens, from the Mohawk poet and nationalist, Emily Pauline Johnson, and from the Sioux teacher and activist, Gertrude Simmons Bonnin whose nationally known lectures and articles characterized Indian rights activity through the forties (68-71,315,483). The fragile thread of interest in Mary Musgrove and in fur trade women appears for the first time, however inaccurately in their first historical incarnations, and however, in Musgrove's case, utterly misunderstood (48,134-35,145,550,659). New types of scholarly work make their bows, edited autobiographies of Crow and Fox women, for example, by the anthropologists Lowie and Michelson (390,437,645).

In the thirties, Ruth Bunzel's landmark study of Zuni taletellers and Pueblo potters began the study of individual, compelling figures which continues to endure today in the affection for "star" artists like Maria Martinez, Pablita Velarde, Nampeyo, and Pitseolak (95-96,282,473,518-19). In this third decade, anthropologists, art historians and collectors alike became smitten with commercially viable Navajo weavers, Pueblo potters, and Apache and Washoe basketmakers. The decade also saw the publication of a few articles on marriage customs, obstetrical-gynecological practices and beliefs, psychopathology, dress and ceremony, and female-centered symbolic life (3,168,216,263,273,616). Studies of the male Plains transvestite tradition actually mentioned similar female traditions, though serious treatment remained unavailable until Jacob's critical re-reading of the literature forty years later (276-77,308). But the thirties initiated trends that later became important areas of study. Margaret Mead's central work, *The Changing Culture Of An Indian Tribe,* demonstrated that a focus on women's roles and the family could be essential to a comprehension of cultural behavior (426). And the first major work on Native women, Ruth Landes' flawed and male-centered *The Ojibwa Woman,* nevertheless introduced to anthropologists the possibility of writing important works on tribal women (370). The "role and status" literature, significant since the early Iroquoian studies of matriorganization, grew with contributions from distinguished scholars writing about previously ignored tribes and male/female role and status contrast studies (111,188-

89,214,271). The autobiographical/biographical literature, by far the sturdiest branch of the scholarly tree, grew healthily in this period (1,49, 383,438-39,473). Besides the now customary ritual dalliance with princesses and saints, historians began to "discover" other women, including poets like the Canadian Mohawk Pauline Johnson, who had engineered and witnessed some of the major events of the tribal past (7,36,59,192-93,198,383,455,541,607). Anthropologists like Ruth Underhill and journalists like Frank Linderman gave us classics on Crow and Papago women, while others wrote of Aleut, Hopi, Southern Cheyenne, and Arapaho women. And the period offered the opening shot in what was defined as Native women's clinical pathologies and social problems. Freud began to join John Smith and the discipline of anthropology as definer of Native women, as a persistent affection for psychoanalysis of Native women appeared (6,149,154,249-50).

The forties offered the now familiar array of psychoanalytic literature, little of it relevant to the health or culture of Native women (46,73,148, 150,152-53). A scattering of biographical and customs-behavior work appeared (15-16,195,402-03,631,666,668-69), and the interest in psychiatric problems shifted, at least in dissertation and thesis work, to a concern for social problems and physical health, as the growth of sociology as a profession inspired scholars to take an interest in juvenile delinquency, unmarried mothers, alcohol abusers and consumers of the Western health care system (528,549,660). The first few articles on physical health grew to postwar baby boom proportions in the sixties and seventies, and when the obstetrical-gynecological literature converted to a focus on fertility and contraceptive behavior, Indians watched with justified suspicion (41-42, 278). An increasing amount of work on female-centered symbolic systems in language and religious belief received interesting treatment in anthropological and folkloric studies in the forties (403,635-36), though such studies never attracted attention as works on matriarchy, infanticide and puberty ceremonies did (209,283,378). The most distinctive works of the war years, however, actually concerned "war work," historic and contemporary (172,275,382). These treatments of Indian women in war work and in traditional Plains warring activity offered pictures of "brave-hearted women" that challenged old stereotypes, but regrettably they were rarely followed up in succeeding years (20,177). Finally, through files begun in the thirties, John Collier, an anthropologist and head of the Bureau of

Indian Affairs, confirmed what we suspected of government attitudes toward Indian women. Architect of the Indian Reorganization Acts which supported tribal men and virtually disenfranchised Indian women through dissolution of their traditional power systems, Collier dealt with Indian women leaders like Alice Lee Jemison in male and non-Native terms (127-28). His misinterpretation of her nationalism, well-documented in his own files, remained uncorrected until Philip's and Hauptman's fine revisionist studies of her and Iroquois nationalism (264-65,502-03).

The favored topics of anthropological writing in the fifties were sexuality, maternal behavior, child-rearing and puberty (41,151,164,222, 272,286,378), while the unresolved arguments on matriarchy, matriliny, and matrifocality continued with unusual vigor (75,363,375,514,521-22). The new work not only added new tribes to those consistently studied, but also began to suggest that matriarchy might have functioned in ways different from the unilateral and simplistic forms understood by earlier scholars. Alas, no resolution to the argument has appeared since these outbursts of the fifties, and vast cultural and political change has rendered most matriarchal systems now amenable only to speculative historical reconstruction. The second major monograph on tribal women, Carma Smithson's *Havasupai Women,* gave the fifties' scholarship its first important work on modernization and forms of retraditionalization (575). Stimulating new autobiographical work on Menominee women and Navajo women undergoing great change opened the now familiar debate over which gender fares better under the stress of change (252,582-83). Historians offered little to the scholarship in this period except some passing and unimportant attention to old heroines, Molly Brant, Sacajawea, Sarah Winnemucca, and Nancy Ward, and to hitherto underdiscussed topics such as women and the fur trade (82,98,103,245,468,529). However, Cherokee historian Carolyn Thomas Foreman gave us the clues to a great many historical women and topics of potential interest in a very badly written but useful book, *Indian Women Chiefs* (196).

It was in the sixties and seventies that significant changes in the literature on Native women began to appear, not only in what was written and how it was interpreted, but most importantly, in who was writing about Indian women. The same old anthropological and social welfare studies of child life and rearing, matrifocality, menstrual taboos, craft, female infanticide and female psychopathology were ever with us (43,

109,220,242,588), but these were greatly enlivened and enriched by studies of education, cultural change, religion, warrior women, taletelling, male and female language and initiation rites (89,177,257,320,330,351,369, 391,405,424,427). Works of anthropologists like Mary Haas and Keith Basso showed sensitivity to Native categories of thought and action, to Native structures of behavior and feeling, symbolic and real (50,246, 543,548,580). The social problems/social welfare literature grew apace with aforementioned suspect attentions to family planning, illigitimacy, alcohol abuse, and unmarried motherhood, but entirely missing in these attentions were Native or tribal definitions of and responses to categories of social behavior (64,289,513).

In two areas, the sixties brought some alteration in content. The decade included vast change for American women, and the call for women's liberation heard in the larger society was paralleled by consciousness raising among Indian women. Demand from Canadian Native women produced the first governmentally-mandated studies of status among Native women. In the first of a series of conference reports sponsored by women's societies, Indian women defined their own problems and began to articulate their own Native and female solutions. These women noted the discriminatory practices which affect their lives—from governmental rules that rob women of tribal status when they marry non-Indian or non-status men to less overt forms of discrimination in education and work. Canada's women first made public themes that were reiterated in their own and US Native women's writing through the seventies and early eighties (8,26,60,140-41,225,372-73,532-33,536,667). Such efforts put Native women squarely in a feminist context, though generally they remained out of contact with non-Indian feminists, and these actions begun in the late sixties continued in the eighties to stir controversy internally in tribes and externally in government. While these early conference reports and essays began a call for female equity, the biographies and autobiographies of the sixties sealed Native women's insistence on recognition of their individuality (227-28, 274,318,371,417,593,604). Familiar names crowded the roll call of authors, but for the first time, Indian and non-Indian writers produced substantive work on Indian women. Ill-written, male-centered and inept interpretations of Native women's lives by mainstream scholars like O'Meara reminded us that much remained to be done (472). But superb works such as the autobiography of Mountain Wolf Woman, presented by a scholar, Nancy Lurie, rightfully respected by Native people, offered a prototype for the future (393). Such work put forward the first real contrast between male and female visions of the world in Indian country, and made later works with their intrusive editors and overdramatized quality seem inferior by comparison. But this work set the stage for important works by Native women, the tales of the healer, Delphina Cuero, or the Christianized Hopi leader, Helen Sekaquaptewa, for example, and made new interpretations of the lives of Native women possible (561,605). Other autobiographies of the period brought illuminated tribal and individual diversity and served as a counter to the large number of male biographies that so compelled readers (56,319,341,390,552). Yet, other autobiographies of the period (Anauta, Winnie, Lone Dog) carried out the firm rules of the Pocahontas Perplex: Indian women have to be exotic, wild, collaborationist, crazy, or white to qualify for white attention (15, 388,625,647). But the beginnings of new approaches to the fur trade and to women's forms of political action made the sixties' promise much (84,178,586).

The seventies bore the fruit of previous generations' seeds. Representing the notion that the study of Indian women was an idea whose time had come was Beatrice Medicine's bibliography on the role of women in Native American societies (432). An outgrowth of one of the first university-based courses on Native women, the bibliography, and succeeding efforts, called attention to the need for work in the field (51,55,232,310,357,387). Subsequently, other works appeared, given impetus by the general American women's movement, but often capitalizing on the strength of the movement without offering the substance demanded by it.

Book-length works brought journalistic pastiches of stories, poems, bits from autobiographies, glossy public-relations-like biographies and no substantive interpretation from Katz, Terrell, and Gridley (238,324,598). A more carefully constructed work by Niethammer synthesizes, often uncritically but comprehensively, material on many aspects of traditional life from standard and obscure anthropological sources (469). Handsomely illustrated, it offers an introduction to traditional life and culture, but nothing on contemporary women. More disappointly, Medicine's *Native American Women: A Perspective* places Indian women in an ethnographic and historical perspective and offers a bare outline critique of scholarly disciplines encased in a discussion of Sioux women (431). But while it makes reference to modern issues like sexual inequity and women in transition, its double-spaced format with pages-long quotations from conventional sources does not give the reader more than an essay-length conversation on problems and solutions.

Some popular photographic essays proffered romanticized portraits of cultural dissolution and change (566,567), but the autobiographies produced in the seventies offer both more substance and more to be corrected than any other genre. Shipek's *Delphina Cuero* underscores, as an autobiography, the changes, disappointments and fulfillments of her fragile tribe's and her own personal existence (561). Another Christianized Hopi, Elizabeth Polingaysi Qoyawayma, deals with a theme quite important to many Native people, working and living in two worlds, in *No Turning Back* (509). And many artists and studies of them recount their artistic and cultural histories as well as their movements from a traditional life into a world of Christianity, whites, museums, and commercial artistry (18,38,123-25,129-30,143,171,271,415,445-46,501,506). As with the story of their archetype, Maria Martinez, it is hard to know in their stories who was the more manipulated and who the cleverest in Indian women's relationships with the white art world. The recently released diaries of yet another artist, Bonita Wa Wa Calachaw Nuñez, a tribal woman adopted at a young age by wealthy New York liberals, will tell readers more about the New York reformist and liberal world than about Native women (587). But Belle Hiwalking's story, commissioned by Native people for educational purposes, gives us the opportunity of hearing from another traditional woman whose vision of change and cultural resistance rings true (280). Quite different from others previously discussed, are the utterly contemporary, harsh tales of Maria Campbell and Bobbi Lee, urban Metis women and the biographical and political story of Anna Mae Aquash, murdered at the second "Battle of Wounded Knee" (76,104,377). Their lives, marred by the hard realities of drugs, booze, poverty, city Indian bars, jails, and violence, and redeemed in modern Indian political activism, give us modern versions of the pasts' brave-hearted women and tell grim stories that rarely pushed the "braids-and-shades"rhetoric of militant Indian men off the front page. We have needed these works along with the other fine autobiographies and biographies of more traditional, more activist, and more deviant women (158,224,268,326-27,401). And we have very much needed the contributions of Jane Kelley's *Yaqui Women,*

Hauptman's revisionist "Alice Lee Jemison," Pandey's "Flora Zuni," and Fowler's "Sarah Winnemucca" as well as other retrospective life-histories and ethnohistorical reevaluations of tribal leaders and women who used their power as agents of change in their beseiged communities (199,264-65,312,331,393,484,462-65,491-92,537,560,615,643).

Besides their work on some autobiographies in these two decades, anthropologists' contributions increased with many useful and interesting items. In more general analyses now available, several authors wrote on Native relations between the sexes and between the races and proffered welcome and revisionist views of Native women and men. Signal to this literature is the superb new body of material on mixed blood and fur trade women, all by female scholars like Van Kirk, Jeffrey, Peterson, and Brown (86-88,313,498,500,609-13). Discarding images of powerless slaves to warriors, children and subsistence life, these and other authors like Schlegel, Kidwell, and Klein portrayed the pervasiveness of powerful roles for women, ones complimentary to those of men. Challenging feminist scholars' insistence on the pervasiveness of male dominance in Native cultures, these writers insisted on tribal rather than Western definitions of roles and status. The literature on culture change was enhanced considerably by several fine works which promoted nonconventional views of what happens to men and women during periods of great cultural change (61,161,243,350,381,414,421-22,447,531,656). Down's analysis, for example, suggested that older models in which women fared better than men during periods of change may not be appropriate when women cannot participate in the positive symbols of change. If the increasing numbers of Native women participating in alcohol abuse or commiting suicide are indicative, Indian women resist or accept change in degrees similar to men. Obviously, work like Downs's should be pursued with the goal of appropriate social action. Finally, tradition, not change, was the favored topic of another group of anthropologists writing about Native women in the seventies. Puberty ceremonies, Inuit infanticide, female socialization, women's speech, female symbolic referents in Native languages, and women's participation in ritual transvestism filled out the forms of cultural analysis in this decade; the latter three topics offer much new substance and interest (116,187,203-05,248,259,269,477,499).

Another body of material bulking large in the seventies and eighties concerned Native women's physical and mental health. While the anthropological literature as definer of Native people is a constant irritant to them, the growing body of medical and psychological studies concerned Native people even more. Since the exposures in the sixties, of sterilization and experimentation abuse on Native American women and men in US Public Health Service facilities, Indian people have been warier than ever of population control and contraceptive technologies (25,155-57,215, 362,448,597,620). Their sense of themselves as test animals for physicians and scientists in need of clinical practice or experimental populations was fueled by an ever-increasing and frequently illuminating literature on fertility, family planning, and contraceptive behavior in Indian populations (244,247,266,358-62,571-72,606,661,663). At the same time, studies which might lead to better health care for Indian women, studies of alcohol abuse, suicide, cancer, and environmental health, for example, either subsume the data for women into those for men or deal with women not at all. Given the rise in morbidity and mortality from alcoholism, suicide, and cervical cancer, and given counseling, intervention, and testing programs directed primarily toward males, Indian women might well wonder whether researchers and clinicians have their best interests at heart. Some clearly do and make protest. Others document the problem, leaving analysis to someone else. Others remain part of the problem (101,345,385,505,603, 619). In mental health programs too, Native women have come increasingly to feel that alien cultural models govern both the understanding of clinical personnel and the therapies directed by them. While the Freudian, psychopathological approach is certainly on the wane, the social problems-counseling models developed for a white majority and Black minority remain favored for Indian women (4,37,63,120,208,317,364,408,420, 442,474,476). As bad as the existence and use of culture-bound, sex-biased studies and therapies has been, worse is the absence of literature which validates and uses traditional Native practice in tandem with useful Western practice. Increasingly, Native women have come to insist on that interface, especially in the inclusion of traditional female healers and herbalists in clinical settings that affect their care (133).

The real flowering of work on Indian women, begun in the late sixties, started to appear in the late seventies and early eighties, and is well-represented in disparate scholarly articles by modern Indian women and non-Indian anthropologists, by revisionist historical writing and modern biography and autobiography, and by Native women leaders and writers talking about their own lives. Many of those writing are not scholars, and they will rarely produce full-length works of classic revisionist scholarship or write for wide audiences. Yet their critique of the scholarship about them, of social action and policy affecting them, and their interpretation of their own experiences are there to examine by scholars and the public (28,112,114,144,296,336 339,530,589-91,602). One only need look at Ruth Roessel's *Women In Navajo Society,* Irene Stewart's *A Voice In Her Tribe,* and the Wheelwright Museum's catalog of their photographic show on Navajo women, curated by Navajo women, to note significant changes. Together with new scholars and new scholarship, and with new works in popular and children's literature, a revised Native woman will appear in the scholarly and public eye (93,139,241,309,357,366-67,511,565, 592,670). In the new literature women show how popular images affect their personal lives as well as delineate limits for realities that affect their collective lives. Others treat of health status, relationships between Indian and non-Indian women and men, the impacts of federal and local governmental statute, culture change, work, education, economics, modern and traditional leadership, and political action and rights. Some of these assessments, like those previous, came out of organized meetings where problems received public analysis (146-47,608). The power of these assessments lies in the persuasiveness of testimony rather than statistical fact and on the uniqueness of the perspectives and interests in contrast with mainstream scholars. I know of no Indian woman preparing systematic studies of puberty rites, for example. Women may believe in them, honor them, and participate in them but, they do not, for the most part, document them or wish to do so. They do not document change; they make change. Their focus remains on strategies to address problems rather than on the descriptive analysis of problems. Overcoming the barriers their status as Indian and female places on them in this world is a theme that runs throughout their words, but an equally strong theme is the advantage of that status. Such words will surprise some who believe that Indian, reservation and female life is burdensome. For example, Canadian Native women try to retain that status when, simply by marrying a non-Indian, they can lose it. It might come as a bigger surprise to many that most Native women look forward to being old, to being a grandmother, to being an elder, when their words, actions and leadership will be respected, even taken for granted. The persistent reference to and honor of grandmothers and the aged throughout their works will support such an insistence, as will new research on the positive aspects of Indian aging (23,329,416, 430,523,556,662,664). These often non-scholarly but very Native female views are expressed in prose and in the recent burst of work by Native women creative writers. Corn Mother, Changing Woman, and Grandmother Turtle, the symbolic referents of Indian female life have, joined with the pow wow princesses and female doctors, lawyers and Indian chiefs in that body of writing to pose a truthful, unromanticized and hardedged version of Native women's lives (12,186,236-37,285,311). It is in all these works that readers may look for the real expression of Native women's lives. It is in these, joined to the new scholarship which often finds strengths in traditional women's networks and sodalities translated into new, often urban forms, that we may look for real revision (35,61, 234,255,435,440-41,461).

In all this political, artistic, and scholarly work by and about Native women, we might well look for the feminist stance, the acknowledgement of political categories of thought and action that everywhere move women scholars and activists. I would insist that such a consciousness, like the overt consciousness and public assertion about Native rights, is there in abundance (19,230-34,303,354,412,475,649-50). Indian women recognize their concerns are similar to those shared by other women, though they would insist, like other Third World women, that they are doubly bound by race and gender. But beyond a rhetorical recognition of the similarities, their writing and public presentation bears little resemblance to conventional feminist analyses of the status and circumstances of women's lives. As an aside, I should also note that the lives of Native North American women have drawn much less scholarly attention from feminists than any other group of Third World women, perhaps because Native women have not revealed themselves to be sympathetic to a feminist analysis any more than to any other kind of analysis. In that spirit, feminist rhetorical consciousness is used, only in part, by Native women to be explanatory and activating, but not to encompass the sum total of interest or concern. Areas of debate such as Marxist, lesbian, socialist, feminist are entirely missing, and I cannot imagine a time when such variants would ever be a part of Indian feminist discussion or a welcomed discussion between Indian and non-Indian women. In fact, given the hostile climate for discussion of any theory applied to Native people, I doubt that feminist theory of any stripe would be well received. For Indian feminists, every woman's issue is framed in the larger context of issues pertinent to Native peoples. The concerns which characterize debate in Indian country, tribal sovereignty and self-determination, for example, put Native people on a collision path with regulations like Title 9, with Equal Opportunity and Affirmative Action. Tribes justly insist that treaty-based sovereignty supercedes any other federal mandate. While many Native women have personal difficulty with the application of tribal sovereignty to affirmative action in tribal hiring, for example, most agree that sovereignty is an issue best debated without exception. Other issues and discussions surrounding them, the need for better health care or for better professional training for women, for instance, always remain rooted in debate over the issues most germane to Indian people—the land, natural resources, water rights, and treaty guarantees (18,34,63-66,78,303,418,467,596,601,632,648,651-53). The ironies multiply when, contrary to standard feminist calls for revolutionary change, Indian women insist on taking their traditional places as healers, legal specialists, and tribal governors. Their call is for a return to forms which, they insist, involve women and men in complementary, mutual roles. I underscore these differences because they may teach us more here than analyses of Indian female "oppression." I am not suggesting that a return to tradition in all its forms would be desirable to all Native women, but rather that attention to debate about the implications of such retraditionalization would mean healthier, more culturally-appropriate scholarship on Native women.

What appears above is a "progress" report on the trends and issues that characterize the literature on and by Native North American women. I have offered some evaluative comments throughout, but a more qualitative analysis is needed if we are to understand, from a scholarly and Native point of view, what has been achieved and what remains for attention. The great preponderance of literature is anthropological and historical in nature. Most of the very good work is by women. And yet, little treats of real Native women or real Native categories of significance. Disciplines have essentially followed their own cues from decade to decade with "primitivism" and popularization as the moving force behind what gets written. The clichéd concerns that every discipline has with women—those stemming primarily from their biological functions as mothers, their social functions as wives or lovers, their economic functions as producers or helpmates—remain the concerns that these disciplines have with Native women. Women as defective beings, psychologically and physically, or as inferior beings, intellectually, socially, politically, yet form the interpretive wrapping within which Native women are bound along with their non-Native female counterparts. Even our "heroines" serve white males, and it is they, not those who fought white males for their children, their land, their relatives and their status, who are beloved. Little is written about the women who most mattered to Native people. For example, apart from the work on Native women as commercial artists and tillers of the cornfield, little exists on them as economic entities and forces, in spite of their frequent and widely occuring status as land holders and property "owners." Though occasional pieces have appeared on medicine women, herbalists, and shamans, they generally ignored the spiritual and medical leadership of these women in favor of "personal" narrative. If we know little about the ways in which the matriarchy functioned in Iroquois daily life, we must suspect that only theory, rather than the actual practice of female decision making, is of interest to scholars. Little wonder that few have written about modern female leadership in tribes which have been female-governed for a long time—Puyallup, Colville, Yavapai, Menominee—or about those women who served as national and tribal political leaders in the last three decades. Little wonder again that a fixation with the traditional evolved into studies of nonthreatening older women, artists and relatives of famous male leaders, rather than into studies of the old women who tell male members of the American Indian Movement what to do in the next militant action. Our picture of how Native women really live and function from the cradle to the grave, especially in a modern context, lacks clarity and realism.

The literature bulks large with studies of the Navajo, the Inuit, Pueblo and Iroquoian groups, with occasional forays into Californian and Ojibwa groups. But where are the women of the Southeast, the Northwest Coast, the Great Plains, and the Siouian peoples whose male counterparts fill the literature on Native people. The choice of tribes and topics shows a distinct preference for those that already interest scholars rather than for those who might offer contradictions to old ideas. Preference continues to be for those people who remain visibly traditional (read: old-fashioned); in trouble (read: dying); amenable to being studied (read: easy to work with); and fit existing models (read: artistic hunter/gatherers). Of course, no tribe has been easy to work with since the late sixties, and many tribes have refused the right to study any aspect of their lives unless those aspects fall into the agendas defined by the tribe itself. Tribes once quite amenable to being research objects are joining tribes never especially hospitable to scholars at all, not even Indian scholars trained in Western forms. Unless that scholarly agenda and approach changes, we will learn less and less about Native women, and there are many things that need to be known in order to make the best of future lives. Even though ridiculously bad works—novels, films, scholarly and popular works—continue to plague us (22,40,85,218,251), we are blessed to be rid, in their former number and nature, of the deviance studies, rug-and-pot articles, and puberty rite descriptions. Yet we long for work that would be of use to Native women as well as to scholars. For example, Indian women and men are not at all very worried about unmarried mothers and illigitimate children, nor about receptivity to family planning services. The growing birthrate among Native peoples is a matter of positive, not negative, concern except where it creates a potential health problem (eg. the high number of teenage mothers). Yet they are terribly concerned about non-Indian adoption of Indian children, child placement programs, potential and real sterilization abuse, clinical experimentation with Indians, missionary activity in schools and tribes, and about the rise in cervical cancer, suicide and diabetes among Indian women. And Indian women are concerned about the future of Indian men and about the grim statistics on their education, employment, familial relationships, legal status, and ability to survive as Indians in this world. Where are the scholars who will lend themselves and their skills to Indian solutions for these concerns? While most of the studies on Pocahontas and her sisters focus on the ways in which they helped non-Indians defeat and subdue their own people, where is the serious study of such women as culture brokers, working to create, manage, and minimize the negative effects of change on their people, working for Native people and with non-Indian women and men? I know of no such study, and I know of only two, both fine, which deal with the strengths of traditional female networks and the resilient pan-Indian or urban networks which keep migratory, urban Indian peoples working, educated and in touch with their Indian identities (435,461). If there are those who recognize the role the Black churches and sororities played in helping Black women survive and grow, where are those who will give the modern versions of Native women's quilling and beading societies—tribal women's groups, pan-Indian and female associations, regional networks, urban Indian centers—the attention they ought to have? The substitution, in these worlds, of blue-jeaned tribal chairwomen for puberty celebrants, dead princesses and prostitutes should benefit Native women and scholars by the introduction of Native women's versions of success and failure.

This review has suggested that resolutions of scholarly questions may be only one sort of legitimate research; that, indeed, scholarly issues may have to be subordinated to community needs when community survival is at stake. Such a suggestion is certainly not a new one in the social sciences, and it most certainly does not preclude the study of older questions. It is simply to say that "studied" peoples may yet demand something of the "student": to cease some kinds of work and undertake others; to tell some stories and wait before telling others; to listen, to hear, instead of talking. Radical scholars, including feminists, have long insisted that all peoples have a right to a personal definition, to an individual agenda apart from that agenda and definition posited in the structures of overt power. It is now time for those scholars to ask Native peoples what their agendas are and how they might lend themselves to the task. Scholars may find that Native questions might give us all better answers, and Native women deserve better questions and better answers, if they are to survive and prosper as individuals and as parts of a collective community. Because so little about Native women has been understood or well-used, even in the massive amount of attention paid to them, they may hold the key to questions and answers about Native people and the human condition that we will all honor in the asking and answering. The promise is there; it need only be kept. Thought Woman thought the world into existence. Changing Woman made it what we now know as the world. Our Beloved Women governed it justly and well. Who will seek and reveal their visions for the future?

Contextual Bibliography

1. Abeita, Louise (Pueblo). *I Am A Pueblo Indian Girl.* New York: William Morrow, 1939.
   A juvenile autobiography, illustrating more of what non-Indians expected from Indians in such works than of what Native women might have had to tell.
2. Aberle, S.B.D. "Child Mortality Among Pueblo Indians." *American Journal Of Physical Anthropology.* 16 (1932): 339-51.
   An historical study of child mortality among Pueblos from the inspection of mortuary remains—lots of speculation about maternal health and nutrition as well as on healing practices and child-rearing.
3. ———. "Maternal Mortality Among the Pueblos." *American Journal Of Physical Anthropology.* 18 (January-March, 1934): 431-35.
   An article which examines the statistics for deaths, death rates and the causes for death among pregnant Pueblo women.
4. Ackerman, Lillian A. "Mental Instability and Juvenile Delinquency Among the Nez Perces." *American Anthropologist.* 73, no.3 (1971): 595-603.
   A description of differential male-female behavior in Nez Perce teenagers deemed to be "disturbed."
5. "Acorns: Staple Foods of California Indians." Produced by Clyde Smith for the Univ. of Cal. Media Extension Center. 16mm. Color/Sound. 28 minutes. 1962.
   A brief, but interesting film on Pomo women and their gathering and preparation of the primary foodstuff, acorns.
6. Adams, Harold E. "Divorce in Primitive Society: A General Survey of the Evolution of Divorce." Dissertation, Yale University, 1929.
   Many tribal customs surrounding divorce surveyed in this early study—fragmentary and rudimentary as a study of Native North American peoples.

7. Adams, Winona. "An Indian Girl's Story of A Trading Expedition to the Southwest About 1841." *The Frontier*. 10 (May, 1930): 338-51, 367.
An unusual account from a woman's perspective—of a very usual enterprise.

8. Alberta Native Women's Society. *First And Second Report*. Edmonton, Alberta: Alberta Native Women's Society, 1968-69.
An early Canadian conference report from women of many tribes, detailing problems Canadian Native women still face in 1980.

9. Alilkatuktuk, Jeela (Inuit). "Canada : Stranger in My Own Land." *Ms. Magazine*. 2, no. 8 (1974): 8-10.
A "between-two-worlds" account of an Inuit woman whose education made her paradoxically fit and unfit to serve her people— one of the few such accounts in a feminist publication.

10. Allen, Elsie (Pomo). *Pomo Basketmaking: A Supreme Art For The Weaver*. Healdsburg, California: Naturegraph Publishers, 1972.
A historical and cultural study on Pomo basketmaking by the famous Pomo weaver, Elsie Allen—appropriate because it tells much about Allen herself—good illustrations and photographs.

11. Allen, Paula Gunn (Laguna Pueblo/Sioux). "Beloved Women: Lesbians in American Indian Culture." *Conditions*. 7 (1981): 67-87.
A highly speculative article, in the absence of much confirming evidence, on the existence and nature of lesbianism in traditional and historical native cultures—equates fear of women's power with putative lesbianism.

12. ———. "The Grace That Remains : American Indian Women's Literature." *Book Forum:* Special Issue on American Indians Today. 13 (1981): 376-83.
A brief look at the kinds and themes of contemporary Native women's literature—relating them both to tradition and change.

13. "The American Indian Oral History Collection Audiotapes." Cassette audiotape, 30 tapes, 2 parts. Produced by Herbert Hoover for Clearwater Publishing Co.
In Part 1, two extensive tapes have material from medicine women as well as men; in part 2, two tapes have a Spokane woman narrating 3 legends and a Sioux mother and daughter speaking about boarding schools.

14. Anahareo, Gertrude Mottke (Cree). *Devil In Deerskins: My Life With Grey Owl.* Toronto: New Press, 1972.

    A highly dramatized tale of a Native woman's marriage with a "white Indian"—their "show business" life—aimed solely at the non-Indian market.

15. Anauta (Inuit) with Heluize C. Washburne. *Children Of The Blizzard.* London: Dennis Dobson, 1960.

    A third revised reprint of an over-romanticized tale by Anauta (Mrs. Fred Blackmore), a very much assimilated and well-known figure in Canada.

16. ———. *Land Of The Good Shadows: The Life Story Of Anauta, An Eskimo Woman.* New York: John Day, 1940; rep. 1976.

    The first edition of a popularized autobiography, done solely for the non-Native market—yet revealing about Inuit life in the early 20th century.

17. Anderson, Marilyn. "The Pocahontas Legend." *The Indian Historian.* 12, no. 2 (1979): 54-59, 64.

    A survey of the Pocahontas tale in literature—somewhat repetitive of major studies—but does list plays, poems in which she appears.

18. Anderson, Owanah (Choctaw), ed. *Resource Guide Of American Indian And Alaskan Native Women.* Newton, Mass.: Women's Educational Equity Action Publishing Center/EDC, 1980.

    Lists the names, occupations, activities, community service action, accomplishments of 500 and more Native women—can be used for evaluation, hiring, assessment of the available pool.

19. ———. *Words Of Today's American Indian Women: Ohoyo Makachi.* Wichita Falls, Texas: Ohoyo Resource Center, 1982.

    This volume contains the edited speeches and discussions of a large number of Native women speakers at a 1981 conference in Tahlequah, Oklahoma—on many topics—status, problems, health, education.

20. Anderson, Robert. "The Northern Cheyenne War Mothers." *Anthropological Quarterly.* 29, no.3 (1956): 82-90.

    A decent, if brief, presentation of the traditional maternal warrior support society with its translation into modern use in World War II and Korea.

21. Anderson, Rufus, transcriber. *Memoirs Of Catherine Brown, Christian Indian Of The Cherokee Nation.* Philadelphia: American Sunday School Union, 1825; rep. 1831.

    A fascinating tale of a planter-class, eastern educated Cherokee woman.

22. Andrews, Lynn V. *Medicine Woman.* San Francisco: Harper and Row, 1981.

    One of the worst books to appear since *Hanta Yo* or the Carlos Casteneda series in terms of phony and stereotyped images of Indians—this of a "medicine woman" who "teaches" a white groupie. Insulting to Indian women.

23. "Annie and the Old One." 16 mm, Color/Sound, 16 minutes, 1976. Produced by Bailey Film Associates.

    A children's film about dealing with the death of a loved person—this one about Annie and her grandmother, traditional Navajos.

24. "Annie Mae: Brave-Hearted Woman." 16mm, Color/Sound, 84 minutes, 1981. Produced by Lan Brookes Ritz for Brown Bird Productions.

    A feature-length film about the work and unexplained murder of Annie Mae Aquash, the Micmac activist involved in Wounded Knee II.

25. Anonymous. "And Then There Were None: IHS Sterilization Practice." *Christian Century.* 94 (January 26, 1977): 61-63.

    One of the many national press articles on the sterilization practices of IHS and the legal actions taken by Native women to reverse the practice.

26. ———. "Canada Confronts A 100 Year Old Injustice." *Ms. Magazine.* 7 (1980): 23.

    A brief article on Canadian Native women's fight to redress the Canadian Indian laws which discriminate, for benefits, against Native women who lose their status if they marry non-status men.

27. ———. "Dakota Images: Ella C. Deloria." *South Dakota History.* (Fall, 1976): 4,6.

    A short biographical sketch of the Sioux anthropologist, educator and linguist who died in 1972.

28. ———. "Female Energy." *Many Smokes.* (Fall, 1981).

Native women from many tribes discuss the essential roles women
played in their cultures.

29. ———. "Hopi Womanpower." *Human Behavior.* 3 (November,
1974): 49-50.
A brief discussion of matrilineality and matriorganization among
the Hopi.

30. ———. "Miss Ann Padlo and Miss Annie Meekitjik." *Canadian
Indians And Eskimos Of Today.* 3, no.4 (1966).
Brief biographical pieces on Canadian Inuit women who are ac-
tivists and community leaders.

31. ———. "Native American Women in Pre-Columbian America."
US History: Teacher Guide And Student Book. Newton, Massachussetts: WEEA Publishing Center, 1980.
A much-improved curricular article written by revisionist scholars—for teachers in secondary institutions.

32. ———. "Return of A Native: A Young Woman Fashions A New
Life From Her Ancestral Past and Discovers A Special Indian
Gift." *Seventeen.* 37 (1978): 94.
A short article on a young woman model and clothes designer.

33. ———. "Sioux Women At Home." *The Illustrated American.* New
York: Bible House/Astor Place, 1891.
An illustrated article on the family life of the Sioux, complete with
drawings and paintings—a Christian view.

34. ———. "Special Issue on Native American Women." *Off Our Backs:
A Magazine Of Women's Liberation.* (February 2, 1981).
Work throughout the issue on the Yvonne Wanrow and Rita Silk-
Nauni criminal conviction cases as well as descriptions of other
areas of political activism by Native women.

35. ———. "A Woman's Ways: An Interview With Judy Swamp."
Parabola. 5, no.4 (1980): 52-61.
An interview with an activist of the Mohawk Longhouse—about
"maintaining traditional values in the context of contemporary
conflict."

36. Apes, William. *The Experiences Of Five Christian Women Of The
Pequod Tribe.* Boston: James Dow, 1933.
A book which offers the testimonies of Christian women from the
Pequod tribe.

37. Armstrong, Robert L. and Barbara Holmes. "Counseling for Socially Withdrawn Indian Girls." *Journal Of American Indian Education.* 10 (January, 1971): 4-7.

    A shallow presentation of counseling strategies for female Indian teenagers who are "withdrawn" from an Anglo perspective of public behavior.

38. Ashton, Robert Jr. "Nampeyo and Lesou." *American Indian Art.* 1, no.3 (1976): 24-34.

    An extended review of the historical contributions of the 19th century Hopi potter, Nampeyo and her husband, Lesou—their pottery styles, technological and design innovations, and artistic legacy.

39. Attneave, Carolyn (Cherokee-Delaware) and Agnes Dill (Isleta Pueblo). "Indian Boarding Schools and Indian Women: Blessing or Curse." In Dpt. of Ed./Nat'l. Inst. of Ed. *Conference On The Educational And Occupational Needs Of American Indian Women, 1976.* Washington, DC: GPO, 1980: 211-31.

    An intriguing reflection on these schools and their effect on Native women.

40. Axtell, James, ed. *The Indian Peoples Of Eastern America: A Documentary History Of The Sexes.* New York: Oxford University Press, 1981.

    A random selection of quotations from European authors and political figures about Indian women, men, domestic relations in the New World.

41. Bailey, Flora L. "Some Sex Beliefs and Practices, Comparative Material From Other Navajo Areas." *Papers Of The Peabody Museum.* 40, no. 2 (1950).

    A completely miscellaneous collection of material, not worth much attention.

42. ———. "Suggested Techniques For Inducing Navajo Women to Accept Hospitalization During Childbirth and for Implementing Health Education." *American Journal Of Public Health.* 38 (October, 1948): 1418-23.

    A work on the improvement of pregnancy outcome through convincing Navajo women to accept Western health care during childbirth.

43. Balikici, Asen. "Female Infanticide on the Arctic Coast." *Man.* 2, no. 4 (1967): 615-25.
An attempt to describe the Inuit practice of killing girl babies.

44. Barbour, Philip L. *Pocahontas And Her World.* New York: Houghton Mifflin, 1970.
One of the standard good biographies of the Princess—with decent primary materials and bibliography—a scholarly treatment.

45. Barker, James N. "The Indian Princess." Philadelphia: American Microprint Collection, 1908.
One of the many early plays about the Princess Pocahontas—quite popular on the stage.

46. Barnouw, Victor. "The Phantasy World of a Chippewa Woman." *Psychiatry.* 12 (1949): 67-76.
A European model of psychiatric analysis transposed onto a Native life—a dream life normal to a traditional person interpreted as "phantasy" by a Western psychiatrist.

47. Barrett, S.M. *Hoistah, An Indian Girl.* New York: Duffield and Company, 1913.
A novel about a nineteenth century Cheyenne woman, based somewhat on fact.

48. Barry, J. Neilson. "Madame Dorion of the Astorians." *Oregon Historical Quarterly.* (September, 1929).
Narrative regarding a well-known female "broker" figure who helped expedite the fur trade empire of John Jacob Astor.

49. Bartram, William. *A Cherokee Daughter Of Mount Holyoke.* Muscatine, Iowa: The Prairie Press, 1937.
A fictionalized biography of an upper-class Cherokee woman educated in the East at Mount Holyoke—interesting for its portrayal of her in this strange world.

50. Basso, Keith. "The Gift of Changing Woman." *Bureau Of American Ethnology Bulletin.* 51, no.196 (1966): 119-73.
A fine symbolic analysis of Navajo and Apache girls puberty rituals—one of the most sensitive treatments.

51. Bataille, Gretchen. "Bibliography on Native American Women." *Concerns.* (Summer, 1980): 16-27.
A bibliography directed primarily toward literature and toward autobiography, expanded from *Medicine*, 1975.

52. Baugh, Timothy Gene. "Dukaksi: The Structural Implications of Matrilateral Cross-Cousin Marriage: The Tlingit Case." Dissertation, University of Oklahoma, 1978.

A structuralist thesis on kinship which, nevertheless, has some very interesting work on matriorganization and matrilineality.

53. Beauchamp, William. "Iroquois Women." *Journal Of American Folklore.* 13 (1900): 81-90.

An early but not very interesting piece on the familiar arguments over Iroquois matriarchy and matriorganization—looks particularly at the mythology.

54. Beckford, Patricia Anne. "A Normative Study of the Physical Fitness of 14, 15 and 16 Year-Old Navajo Girls Using the AAHPER Youth Fitness Test." Thesis, North Texas State University, 1976.

A study which measures physical fitness of Navajo girls according to a standardized test.

55. Beidler, Peter J. and Marion F. Egge. *The American Indian In Short Fiction: An Annotated Bibliography.* Metuchen, NJ and London: The Scarecrow Press, 1979.

A bibliography which lists hundreds of stories with Indians as their topic, quite of few of which have female subjects—some Native authors (Leslie Silko, Ted Williams, Charles Eastman) and non-Native (Harte, Hemingway).

56. Bennett, Kay (Navajo). "Kaibah" and "Songs From the Navajo Nation by Kaibah." LP and 8-Track Recordings from Canyon Records, c. 1975.

Traditional and modern songs from the Navajo writer and actress, Kay Bennett—good on some of the traditional songs.

57. ———. *Kaibah, Recollections Of A Navajo Girlhood.* Los Angeles: Westernlore Press, 1964.

An interesting, but somewhat romanticized tale of a traditional childhood—by a singer and entertainer now living an urban life—one keeps wishing for the next half to be told for balance.

58. Bernstein, Alison R. "Outgrowing Pocahontas: Toward A New History of Indian Women." *Minority Notes.* (Spring-Summer, 1981): 3-8, 31.

A survey of women's stereotypes, a critique of scholarship and methodology, and suggestions for remedying scholarly work.

59. Bighead, Kate, as told to Thomas Marquis. "She Watched Custer's Last Battle: The Story of Kate Bighead." Hardin, Montana: privately printed by Thomas Marquis, 1933.

A very useful, interesting story—though interpreted by a reporter—of a Crow woman witness to the battle at Little Big Horn.

60. Bird, Florence (Cree) et al. "Native Women in the North." In *Report Of The Royal Commission On The Status Of Women.* Ottawa: Royal Commission on the Status of Women, 1970: 210-17.

A status report on Canadian Native women—good comparative information—working in a multi-tribal collective effort.

61. Blanchard, Evelyn Lance (Pueblo). "Organizing American Indian Women." In: Dpt. of Ed./Nat'l Inst. of Ed. *Conference On The Educational And Occupational Needs Of American Indian Women, 1976.* Washington, DC: GPO, 1980: 123-41.

An examination of appropriate leadership styles and organizations.

62. Blanchard, Kendall. "Changing Sex Roles and Protestantism Among the Navajo Women in Ramah." *Journal For The Scientific Study Of Religion.* 14 (March, 1975): 43-50.

A challenging piece on culture change and religion among Navajo women in an outlying Navajo community—interesting for its perspective on the role of conversion in adaptation to change.

63. Bloom, Joseph D. "Migration and the Psychopathology of Eskimo Women." *American Journal Of Psychiatry.* 110, no. 4 (1973): 446-49.

A conventional psychiatric exploration into the psyches of Inuit women with migratory life cycles—attributes more to traditional migration than it merits.

64. Bock, Philip K. "Patterns of Illegitimacy On A Canada Indian Reserve." *Journal Of Marriage And The Family.* 26 (May, 1964): 448.

Illegitimacy is defined completely from an Anglo perspective even though the author perceives some Native categories.

65. Bomberry, Dan, ed. "Sage Advice From a Long Time Activist: Janet McCloud." *Native Self-Sufficiency.* 6 (1981): 4-5, 20.

An interview with the Tulalip activist, Janet McCloud, a prime mover in the fishing rights cause on the Northwest Coast—some comments about the roles of women.

66. Bomberry, Victoria. "Navajo Organizer Leads Fight Against Uranium." *Native Self-Sufficiency.* 6 (1981): 16-17.
An interview with Emma Peshlakai about her role and the activities in the fight against energy development—and the resultant health and social problems—in the Southwest.

67. Bonney, Rachel A. "The Role of Women in Indian Activism." *Western Canadian Journal Of Anthropology.* 6 (1976): 243-48.
A relatively unsophisticated analysis of how women function in mainstream Indian organizations and in activities directed toward Indian causes.

68. Bonnin, Gertrude Simmons (Sioux). "An Indian Teacher Among Indians." *Atlantic Monthly.* 85 (March, 1900): 381-86.
Details Zitkala-sa's experiences as a teacher in the Dakotas—the valuable perspective of an educated woman turned activist and political leader.

69. ———. "Impressions of an Indian Childhood." *Atlantic Monthly.* 85 (January, 1900): 34-47.
One of a series of articles by Bonnin (Zitkala-sa) in which she recounts her growing up—good for Sioux child-rearing information, but better for Bonnin's recall of it to a non-Indian audience.

70. ———. "Schooldays of an Indian Girl." *Atlantic Monthly.* 85 (February, 1900): 185-94.
Bonnin's tale of the education she received at the hands of Catholic teachers in the Dakotas—valuable for its interpretation of the uses and abuses of education for Native children.

71. ———. "Why I Am A Pagan." *Atlantic Monthly.* 90 (1902): 801-03.
The most interesting of Zitkala-sa's autobiographical articles in many ways—where she explains her return to Native religious belief and culture after her European and Catholic education.

72. Boudinot, Elias (Cherokee). *Poor Sarah, Or The Indian Woman.* New Echota, Georgia: Privately printed, 1817.

A bilingual text in Cherokee and English by this Cherokee intellectual leader—the novel is unremittingly Christian and European, but interesting because of its presentation by a Native man.

73. Bourguignon, Erika. "A Life History of An Ojibwa Young Woman." In Bert Kaplan, ed. *Primary Records In Culture And Personality.* Madison, Wisconsin: Microcard Foundation, 1949.

A psychiatric perspective, quite unnecessary, on an otherwise interesting and useful personal account.

74. Bowman, John Clarke. *Powhatan's Daughter.* New York: Viking Press, 1973.

One of the many literary treatments about Pocahontas—this one no more interesting than the others.

75. Boyer, Ruth M. "The Matrifocal Family Among the Mescalero: Additional Data, Part 1." *American Anthropologist.* 66 (1964): 593-602.

Notes toward a description of matriorganization among the Mescalero Apache—little depth, but good basic data.

76. Brand, Johanna. *The Life And Death Of Anna Mae Aquash.* Toronto: James Larimer and Co., 1978.

An unusual and well-written story of Anna Mae Aquash, mysteriously murdered by unknown assailants during the battle of Wounded Knee II—the story of women in the movement.

77. Braudy, Susan. "Buffy St. Marie: 'Native North American Me.'" *Ms. Magazine.* 4 (March, 1975): 14-18.

A nice piece on the art and political activity of the well-known Cree singer.

78. ———. "We Will Remember Survival School: The Women and Children of the American Indian Movement." *Ms. Magazine.* 5 (July, 1976): 94-120.

A brief article on the alternative schools set up by AIM women in South Dakota and their roles in activist movements.

79. Briggs, Jean L. "Eskimo Women: Makers of Men." In C.J. Matthiasson, ed. *Many Sisters: Women In Cross-Cultural Perspective.* New York: The Free Press, 1974: 261-304.

A look at the roles women play in determining roles of men.

80. ———. "Kaplunga Daughter: Living With Eskimos." *Transaction.* 7, no. 8 (1970): 12-24.

One of many works on whites who lived among the Inuit, this one commenting on sex roles, and rising above the genre to some extent.

81. Brill, A.A. "Pibloktoq, or Hysteria Among Peary's Eskimos." *Journal Of Nervous And Mental Disorders.* 40 (1913): 514-20.

A very dated presentation, from a Freudian perspective, of a native mental disorder among "Peary's" Eskimos.

82. Brimlow, George. "The Life of Sarah Winnemucca: The Formative Years." *Oregon Historical Quarterly.* 53 (June, 1952): 103-34.

An article representing some renewed interest in Winnemucca, though filled with as much speculation as fact. Looks at influences on Winnemucca's political consciousness.

83. Brindley, W.E. "Sacajawea, Tardy Hour For A Neglected Heroine." *Historical Society Of Montana.* 7 (1910).

A mundane memorial piece on the erection of a statue to the Lewis and Clark guide.

84. Broussard, C. "Mohawk Beauty With A Mission." *Look.* 28 (January, 1969): 91-94.

A popular article about the political activism of model educator Kahn Tineta Horn—in Canada and the U.S.

85. Brown, Dee. *Creek Mary's Blood.* New York: Holt, Rinehart and Winston, 1980.

A fictional treatment combining the lives of Mary Musgrove and Nancy Ward—where Brown tries to inject all of Indian history after Removal into the potentially fascinating story of a strong female leader—a bad effort.

86. Brown, Jennifer S.H. "Changing Views Of Fur Trade, Marriage, and Domesticity: James Hargrave, His Colleagues and 'The Sex.' " *Western Canadian Journal Of Anthropology.* 6 (1976): 92-105.

A superb article preceding Brown's equally good book (1981) on the fur trade relationships between white men and Indian women.

87. ———. "Company and Native Families: Fur Trade Social and Domestic Relations in Canada's Old Northwest." Dissertation, University of Chicago, 1976.

The dissertation precursor to Brown's useful book (1981) on relations between Native women and fur trade men.

88. ———. *Strangers In Blood: Fur Trade Families In Indian Country.* Vancouver, Canada and London: University of British Columbia Press, 1981.

A very fine work on the marital and social relations of Native women, British and French male fur traders, their families, incoming British women, and the fur trade itself.

89. Brown, Judith K. "A Cross-Cultural Study of Female Initiation Rites." *American Anthropologist.* 65 (1963): 837-53.

A very worthwhile comparison of initiation ceremonies with quite a bit about American Native peoples.

90. ———. "Economic Organization and the Position of Women Among the Iroquois." *Ethnohistory.* 17, no.3-4 (Summer-Fall, 1970): 151-67.

One of the several modern revisionist articles on the Iroquois matriarchy which suggests that their high status and power was attributable to their control over economic (agricultural) resources.

91. Brown, Marion Marsh. *Homeward, The Arrow's Flight.* Nashville, Tennessee: The Abington Press, 1980.

A juvenile biography of the Omaha physician and activist, Suzanne LaFlesche—a decent effort.

92. Bryant, Loy Y. "The Pocahontas Theme in American Literature." Thesis, University of North Carolina, 1930.

One of the very many treatments of the Pocahontas story in literature.

93. Buckley, Thomas. "Menstruation and the Power of Yurok Women: Methodology in Cultural Reconstruction." *American Ethnologist.* 9, no.1 (1982): 47-60.

A proposed method for investigating the position of women and the aboriginal role of menstruation in culture—very good.

94. Buehrle, Marie Cecilia. *Kateri Of The Mohawks.* Milwaukee: Bruce Publishing Co., 1954.

A children's religious biography of the Mohawk "saint."

95. Bunzel, Ruth. *The Pueblo Potter.* New York: Columbia University Press, 1929; rep. 1972.

The classic work on the female Pueblo potters from San Ildefonso and their families—the opening shot in the Maria Martinez cult—still a relevant work, though dated.

96. ———. *Zuni Texts.* New York: G.E. Steckert and Company, 1933.

Flora Zuni, Linda Zuni and other female members of the tribe offer traditional narratives along with a superb autobiography of Linda Zuni.

97. Bureau of Indian Affairs. *Indian Record:* Special Issue on Indian Women. (February, 1969).

An innocuous and fairly insubstantial report on Native women in federal tribes.

98. Burns, Annie Walker. *Military And Genealogical Record Of The Famous Indian Women Of Tennessee.* Washington, DC: privately printed ms. 1957.

An eccentric, brief notation about potentially interesting people.

99. Burt, Olive Wooley. *Sacajawea.* New York: Watts, 1978.

A very minor popular piece about the Shoshone guide.

100. Burton, Jimalee (Cherokee). *Indian Heritage, Indian Pride.* Norman: University of Oklahoma Press, 1974.

An autobiography of sorts, interlaced with folktales, native beliefs—some Cherokee material—speeches and statements about Indian culture.

101. Butte, Mary Felicia. "The Interrelationship of Nutritional State and Lactational Performance." Dissertation, University of California, 1980.

An examination of the relationship between pre-natal and after-birth nutrition and breast-feeding capabilities of Navajo women.

102. California Urban Indian Health Council. *California Indian Maternal And Child Health Plan.* Oakland, CA: California Urban Indian Health Council, 1982.

Status, policy and an analysis of morbidity and mortality rates of California Native women and children—a proposed plan to remedy bad state of their health care.

103. Campbell, Majorie Wilkins. "Her Ladyship, My Squaw." *The Beaver.* (Autumn, 1954): 14-17.

A brief article describing the awkward social relationships between fur trade men, their women—Native and non-Native, and those women.

104. Campbell, Maria (Metis). *The Half-Breed.* Toronto: McClelland and Stewart, 1973.

A "between-two-worlds" autobiography by a Metis woman who details her traditional and urban life through poverty, alcohol, and rage—especially good for the political and cultural analysis of her life.

105. Capps, Benjamin. *A Woman Of The People.* New York: Fawcett, 1966.

The all-too-familiar tale of the white female captive who "becomes" Indian and a leader of "her" people.

106. Carius, Helen (Inuit). *Sevukamet: Ways Of Life On St. Lawrence Island, Remembrances Of Helen Carius, Inuit* (Slkwooho). Anchorage: Alaska Humanities Forum, 1979.

The remembrances of a traditional Inuit woman, about a traditional Inuit life—a valuable recounting.

107. Carr, Lucien. "On the Social and Political Position of Women Among the Huron-Iroquois Tribes." *Sixteenth Annual Report Of The Peabody Museum Of Archaeology And Ethnology.* 3 (1884-87): 207-32.

The opening shot in the arguments on the Iroquois matriarchy.

108. Cassadore, Patsy. "I Build the Wickiup And Other Apache Songs." LP Recording from Canyon Record, c. 1975.

A very fine recording by Patsy Cassadore and other traditional Apache women singers—a good selection of women's songs.

109. Chance, Norman and Dorothy A. Foster. "Symptom Formation and Patterns of Psychopathology in a Rapidly Changing Alaskan Eskimo Society. *Anthropological Papers Of The University Of Alaska.* 7, no.1 (1962): 32-42.

An attempt to document the stresses of change among Inuit peoples.

110. Chauchétière, Claude. "The Life of the Good Katherine Tegaguita, Now Known As the Holy Savage." Montreal: Archives of St. Mary's College ms., 1685-1695.

One of the original accounts by a priest, of the "Lily of the Mohawks"—made legendary and essential to Indian folk Catholicism in this important record.

111. The Child Study Association of America. *The Indian Girl: Her Social Heritage, Her Needs And Opportunities.* Washington, DC: Government Printing Office, 1934.
A very dated study of Indian girls, setting out her putative problems in educational settings.

112. "Children of Changing Woman: Myth, Symbol and Navajo Women." A catalog, with narrative, of an exhibition of photographs, at the Wheelwright Museum (Museum of Navajo Ceremonial Art), 1977.
A beautiful exhibition catalog from an exhibit of photographs—many photographers, some Navajo women—documenting the daily and ceremonial life of traditional Navajo women.

113. Choulenc, Peter. S.J. *The Life Of Katherine Tehahourtha, First Iroquois Virgin.* Montreal: Archives of St. Mary's College ms., 1696.
More of what is found in the earlier Chauchétière manuscript—somewhat more illuminating about early Jesuit missionary work in Canada than about the subject.

114. Christensen, Rosemary (Chippewa). "Indian Women: A Historical and Personal Perspective." *Pupil And Personnel Services Journal.* 4, no. 5 (1975): 13-22.
A discussion of overcoming stereotypes and functioning as both a tribal and professional woman in the education professions.

115. Clark, Ella Elizabeth and Margot Edmonds. *Sacajawea Of The Lewis And Clark Expedition.* Berkeley: University of California Press, 1980.
A superb book detailing the steps of the Lewis and Clark expedition and placing the Shoshone guide in the historical perspective that she has deserved.

116. Clark, LaVerne Harrell. "The Girl's Puberty Ceremony of the San Carlos Apaches." *Journal Of Popular Culture.* 10 (Fall, 1976): 431-48.
A fairly shallow treatment of the ever-popular topic.

117. Clarke-Smith, Linda. "Primitive Women: A Study of Women Among the Tribes of Australia and of the Iroquois Confederacy." Thesis, Columbia University, 1907.

The usual early comparative study, library-based and unenlightening.

118. Clifford, Myrtle. *Three Women Of Frontier Montana.* Montana: privately printed ms., 1930.

One Indian woman's personal account amongst the three pieces.

119. Clift, Edith Connelly. "Sacajawea, Guide to the Lewis and Clark Expedition." *Prairie Lore.* (April, 1933): 194.

A very brief biographical sketch with little new information.

120. Clinton, Lawrence and Bruce Chadwick and Howard M. Bahr. "Vocational Training for Indian Migrants: Correlates of 'Success' in a Federal Project." *Human Organization.* 32, no. 1 (1973): 17-27.

Quite a bit on Native women in this article, unusual because it focuses on success strategies rather than pathology and failure.

121. Clough, Wilson D. "Mini-Aku: Daughter of Spotted Tail." *Annals Of Wyoming.* 39 (1967): 187-216.

A popularized biography of a young woman interesting to this author only because she was Spotted Tail's daughter.

122. Cohen, Leonard. *Beautiful Losers.* New York: Viking Press, 1966.

A very fictional treatment of the life of Kateri Tekakwitha, the Mohawk "saint," where she becomes the metaphor for the Canada that might have been—a beautiful book and an unusual use of Native women as metaphor.

123. Cohodas, Marvin. "Dat so la lee's Basketry Design." *American Indian Art.* 1, no. 4 (1976): 22-31.

A good study of the premier Washoe artisan, the innovator in design, Dat so la lee.

124. ———. "Lena Frank Dick: Washoe Basket Maker." *American Indian Art Magazine.* 4, no. 4 (1979): 32-41.

A detailed appreciation of this master basketmaker whose designs changed Washoe tradition.

125. ———. "Sarah Mayo and Her Contemporaries: Representational Designs In Washoe Basketry." *American Indian Art.* (Autumn, 1981): 52-59.

A detailed examination of the contributions of Sarah Mayo and other Washoe basketmakers to change and design in new basketry.

126. "Colliding Worlds." 16mm, Color/Sound, 1981. Produced by Orie Sherman (Mono) and distributed, Sherman.

    A film that depicts three generations of Mono women in their relationships to tradition and change.

127. Collier, John. "Alice Lee Jemison." *Office Files Of John Collier, RG75:* Princeton University Library, 1940.

    A brief, but slanderous outpouring of scorn on Jemison from the Commissioner of Indian Affairs—indications of the complete misunderstanding Collier had of the Seneca nationalist.

128. ———. "Memorandum on Indian Women." American Civil Liberties Union Archives: Princeton University Library, 1940.

    Another mysogynist view on Indian women from the former head of the BIA—a dim view of their political activities.

129. Collings, Jerold L. "Profile of a Chemehuevi Weaver." *American Indian Art Magazine.* 4, no. 4 (1979): 60-67.

    Though very much directed toward the collector, this article is a decent description of an art form from a tribe rarely attended to in art circles.

130. Collins, John E. *Nampeyo, Hopi Potter: Her Artistry And Legacy.* Fullerton, California: Muckenthaler Cultural Center, 1974.

    A retrospective catalog, from an exhibition, on the 19th century revitalization and refinement of Hopi pottery by Nampeyo, the extraordinary designer and potter.

131. Colson, Elizabeth, ed. *Autobiographies Of Three Pomo Women.* Berkeley: University of California Archaeological Research Facility, 1974.

    Detailed, moving narratives from three strong women—Sophie Martinez, Jane Adams, Ellen Wood—and their acute perceptions of their lives as Pomo women.

132. Comer, NA. "Hokahe! Look At the Young Indian Woman." *Mademoiselle.* 71 (October, 1970): 158-59.

    A brief look at a model and fashion-conscious young Indian woman with high professional ambitions.

133. Cook, Katsi (Mohawk). "The Women's Dance: Reclaiming Our Powers on the Female Side of Life." *Native Self-Sufficiency.* 6 (1981): 17, 18-19.

An article, abstracted from a longer piece, on the rediscovery and redirection of Native women's health through a reaffirmation of women's traditional status and power.

134. Corry, John Pitts. "Some New Light On the Bosomworth Claims." *Georgia Historical Quarterly.* 25 (1941): 195-224.

An article succeeding Coulter (1927), which suggests that Mary Matthews Musgrove Bosomworth, leader of the Creeks during colonization, may not have been the self-serving leader Coulter found.

135. Coulter, E. Merton. "Mary Musgrove, Queen of the Creeks: A Chapter of Early Georgia Troubles." *The Georgia Historical Quarterly.* 11, no. 1 (1927): 1-30.

The major article on Mary Matthews Musgrove Bosomworth—the controversial and fascinating "broker" figure who worked and fought between the Creeks and Oglethorpe's colonists—takes the view that Mary fought for her own benefit.

136. Council on Interracial Books for Children. *Stereotypes, Distortions And Omissions In US History Textbooks.* New York: Council on Interracial Books for Children, 1977.

Some information on the treatment of Native women included in the general examination of textbooks and the image of women, minorities.

137. Cox, Gail Diane. "An American Princess in London." *American History Ilustrated.* (October, 1978).

A work on the many paintings and illustrations inspired by Pocahontas' visit to England.

138. Crawford, Helen. "Sakajawea." *North Dakota Historical Quarterly.* 1 (April, 1927).

One of the many articles on the guide/translator for Lewis and Clark—not so useful.

139. Cruikshank, Julie. "Athapaskan Women: Lives and Legends." *Canadian Ethnology Service Paper:* Nat'l. Museum of Man. 57 (1979).

Some interview material and some brief biographies of Athapaskan women.

140. ———. "Native Women in the North." *North*/Nord. 18, no. 6 (1971): 1-7.

A brief appreciation of the steps Canadian Native women take to increase their participation in social and economic change.

141. ———. "The Role Of Northern Canadian Indian Women in Social Change." Thesis, University of British Columbia, 1978.

One of several works by Cruikshank on Native women in Canada—this one involved in an examination of their active role in accepting and engineering change.

142. Crying Wind (Kickapoo). *Crying Wind.* Chicago: Moody Press, 1977.

The autobiography of an artist—a spiritual and Christian story.

143. Culley, LouAnn Faris. "Helen Hardin: A Retrospective." *American Indian Art Magazine.* (Summer, 1979): 68-75.

About the contemporary painter, Pablita Velarde's daughter, and the complex transformations of traditional themes and techniques that characterize her work—an appreciation primarily for collectors.

144. Deer, Ada (Menominee) with R.E. Simon, Jr. *Speaking Out.* Chicago: Children's Press Open Door Books, 1970.

A story of Deer's childhood, her professional education as a social worker, and her rise to political consciousness and leadership in the Menominee restoration efforts after tribal termination.

145. Defenbach, Byron. *Red Heroines Of The Northwest.* Boston: Caxton Printers, 1929.

An Anglo male view of who constitutes a heroine—mostly women like Chipeta who saved white people from "savage" Indians.

146. Department of Labor/Women's Bureau. "American Indian Women." Washington, DC: Government Printing Office, 1977.

A four page summary of work, educational and employment status.

147. ———. *Native American Women In Equal Opportunity.* Washington, DC: Government Printing Office, 1979.

A report based on a meeting held in Washington—on the employment and economic status of Native women in the government and labor force—recommendations.

148. Devereaux, George. "The Function of Alcohol in Mohave Society." *Quarterly Journal For Studies On Alcohol.* 9 (September, 1948): 207-51.

Some interesting information on sex-role differences on alcohol use, though a naive view of alcohol use in general.

149. ———. "Institutionalized Homosexuality of the Mohave Indians." *Human Biology.* 9 (1937): 498-527.
Though tiresome for its rigid Freudian interpretation, this article does depart from the customary fascination with the Plains berdache to offer information on female transsexual behavior.

150. ———. "Mohave Indian Obstetrics: A Psychoanalytic Study." *American Imago.* 5 (July, 1948): 95-139.
A Freudian analysis of obstetrical practices, valuable only for its description of those practices.

151. ———. "Mohave Indian Verbal and Motor Profanity." *Psychoanalysis And The Social Sciences.* 3 (1951): 99-127.
Devereaux' usual Freudian analysis tacked onto traditional Mohave verbal expression, some of which is obscene and a great deal of which is used by women.

152. ———. "Mohave Orality: An Analysis of Nursing and Weaning Customs." *Psychoanalytic Quarterly.* 16 (1947): 519-46.
Interesting for its comments on behavior that might be of modern concern for nutrition and health, but not for its comments on Mohave psychology.

153. ———. "Mohave Pregnancy." *Acta Americana.* 6, no. 1-2 (1946): 89-116.
Devereaux's usual Freudian analysis of Native behavior—this work on pregnancy and the beliefs that accompany it.

154. ———. "The Sexual Life of the Mohave Indians: An Interpretation in Terms of Social Psychology." *Human Biology.* 9, no. 4 (1937): 498-527.
One of Devereaux's initial attempts at describing the sexual behavior of tribal peoples—cannot be taken seriously.

155. Dillingham, Brint. "Indian Women and IHS Sterilization Practices." *American Indian Journal.* 3, no. 1 (January, 1977): 27-28.
One of the first reports in this journal devoted to legal issues involving Indians on the increasing critical examination of sterilization practices in Indian Health Service.

156. ———. "Sterilization: A Conference and a Report." *American Indian Journal.* 4, no. 1 (January, 1978): 13-16.

An update on the many activities undertaken by Indian activists and advocates to address the issue of sterilization in Indian health care institutions.

157. ———. "Sterilization Update." *American Indian Journal 3, no.* 9 (September, 1977): 25.

A follow-up to a previous article on sterilization and Indian Health Service.

158. Dominguez, Chona (Cahuilla). In H. Seiler, ed. *Cahuilla Texts.* Indiana University Language Science Monographs 6 (1970): 148-52.

A brief narrative of "bygone days"—moving from a woman of a tribe much reduced in numbers and much threatened by culture change and land loss.

159. Doran, Christopher M. "Attitudes of 30 American Indian Women Toward Birth Control." *Health Service Reports.* 87, no. 7 (1972): 658-64.

An attitude survey, done with women of a number of tribes, about their feelings toward contraception and various methods of contraception.

160. Douglas, Frederic H. *Indian Women's Clothing And Fashion: Function And Basic Types Of Indian Women's Costumes.* Denver, CO: Denver Art Museum Leaflet, 1950.

A review, fairly shallow, of types of women's clothing, mostly Plains.

161. Downs, James L. "The Cowboy and the Lady: Models As A Determinant of the Rate of Acculturation Among the Pinon Navajo." In Howard M. Bahr et al, eds. *Native Americans Today: Sociological Perspectives.* New York: Harper and Row, 1972: 275-90.

A truly interesting work on culture change, challenging the notion that women fare better than men during periods of great change.

162. "Dream Dances of the Kashia Pomo." 16mm, Color/Sound, 30 minutes, 1964. Produced by W.R. Heick for the Univ. of Cal. Media Extension Ctr.

A fascinating, but overlong film, about the women's dream dances inspired by the female healer's dreams and Christian tradition.

163. Driver, Harold E. "Cultural Element Distributions: Sixteen Girls' Puberty Rites in Western North America." *Comparative Studies*

By Harold Driver And Essays In His Honor. New Haven: Human Relations Area Files Press, 1974.

A classic work on traits (e.g. a foot race) during puberty ceremonies.

164. ———. "Girls' Puberty Rites in Western North America." *University Of California Anthropological Records.* 6 (1950): 21-90.

A descriptive ethnography, brief in every case, of Southwestern ceremonies—not the best descriptions available.

165. ———. "A Reply to Opler on Apachean Subsistence, Residence and Girls' Puberty Rites." *American Anthropologist.* 74 (1972): 1147-51.

A disagreement over Opler's (Opler, 1972) attempt to connect residential patterns, economic and ceremonial behavior.

166. Driver, Harold E. and Saul Riesenberg. "Hoof Rattles and Girls' Puberty Rites in North and South America." *Indiana University Publications In Anthropology And Linguistics.* (1960).

One of Driver's several short pieces on trait distribution in puberty ceremonies, descriptive but struggling toward theory.

167. Drury, Clifford. "Sacajawea's Death, 1812 or 1884?" *Oregon Historical Quarterly.* 5 (1955).

One of the many unenlightening disputes over when and where she died.

168. DuBois, Cora. "Girls' Adolescence Observances in North America." Dissertation, University of California, 1932.

A soon-to-be well-known anthropologist's thesis on puberty rites—one of the first major attentions, though not of special interest now.

169. Dunn, Dorothy. "Pablita Velarde, Painter of Pueblo Life." *El Palacio.* 59 (1952): 335-41.

A nice early account of the work and influence of the well-known Pueblo painter who began the contemporary Pueblo painting tradition.

170. Durham, Marilyn. *The Man Who Loved Cat Dancing.* New York: Dell Publishers, 1972.

More about the frontiersman who loved her than about Cat Dancing, the beautiful Indian woman who, to no one's surprise, meets a tragic end.

171. Eagleday, John. "Artist Profile: Estella Loretto." *Four Winds: The International Forum For Native American Art, Literature And History*. (Summer-Autumn, 1981): 10-15.
     An appreciation, by her husband, of the Jemez potter-sculptor of female figures.

172. Eckert, Bertha M. *An Unpublished Report On Indian Women Workers In The War Industries*. New York: Young Women's Christian Association, 1943.
     An obscure but valuable piece on war work—an important aspect of women's activities in traditional and new contexts.

173. Elliott, Karen Sue. "The Portrayal of the American Indian Woman in a Select Group of American Novels." Dissertation, University of Minnesota, 1979.
     A rather ordinary study of the Indian woman's use and image in American literature.

174. Elliott, T.C. "The Grave of Madame Dorion." *Oregon Historical Quarterly*. (March, 1935).
     Yet another speculative and unimportant piece on where some historical figure was buried.

175. "Eskimo Artist: Kenojuak." 16mm, Color/Sound, 20 minutes, c.1970. Produced by Tom Daly for the National Film Board of Canada. Shows the now well-known stone lithographic print techniques of this Inuit artist, Kenojuak—a good film on an artist.

176. Ewers, John C. "Climate, Acculturation and Costume: A History of Women's Clothing Among the Indians of the Southern Plains." *Plains Anthropologist*. 25, no. 87 (1980): 63-82.
     A very interesting article connecting adaptation to cultural and ecological environments with the development of clothing styles.

177. ———. "Deadlier Than the Male." *American Heritage*. 16, no. 4 (1965): 10-13.
     A brief, popularized and entertaining, but very male view, on aggressive and warring behavior among Native women from many tribes.

178. ———. "Mothers of the Mixed Bloods: The Marginal Woman in the History of the Upper Missouri." In Kenneth Ross Toole, ed. *Probing The American West*. Santa Fe: Museum of New Mexico, 1962.

A useful focus on the mothers, but superceded by better, unbiased work.

179. Eymar, Francis. "The Teshoa, A Shoshonean Woman's Knife: A Study of American Indian Chopper Industries." *Pennsylvania Archaeology.* 34 (1968): 9-52.

Interesting only because it focuses on tools made by women for women's work.

180. Fagin, Kay Kelly. "Matrifocality in a Contemporary Cheyenne Community." Dissertation, University of Oklahoma, 1978.

A very traditional anthropology thesis on matriorganization in a "patriarchal" tribe.

181. Farrer, Claire. "Mescalero Apache Girl's Puberty Ceremonies." In Charlotte J. Frisbie, ed. *Southwest Indian Ritual Drama.* Albuquerque: University of New Mexico Press, 1980.

A decent and thorough ethnographic description of the much-studied rite—from a "women's culture" and a "performance" perspective.

182. Fink (Dozier), Marianne A. "Personality Difficulties of Acculturation in Navajo Adolescent Girls As Revealed by the Rorschach Test." Thesis, University of New Mexico, 1950.

A highly speculative and frail thesis on acculturation based on interpretations of Rorschachs.

183. Finney, Frank F. Sr. "Maria Tallchief in History: Oklahoma's Own Ballerina." *Chronicles Of Oklahoma.* 38 (Spring, 1960): 8-11.

A brief biographical remembrance of the Osage prima ballerina—along with something on her family.

184. "First Americans; Marie Potts." Videotape Series, B and W, c.1970. Produced by the Office of Cultural Education , State Univ. of NY.

One film in a series on contemporary Indians features Marie Potts, a Maidu cultural leader, discussing history, legends, politics.

185. Fischer, LeRoy H. "Muriel H. Wright: Historian of Oklahoma." *Chronicles Of Oklahoma.* (Spring, 1974): 3-21.

An appreciation of Wright, one of the major chroniclers of Oklahoma Indian history and an Indian rights advocate—along with a bibliography of her works.

44 *Contextual Bibliography*

186. Fisher, Alice Poindexter. "The Transportation of Tradition: A Study of Zitkala-sa and Mourning Dove, Two Transitional American Indian Writers." Dissertation, City University of New York, 1979.
    A study of two of the first "professional" American Indian women writers, the author of *Cogewea* and the activist and educator—a good effort.
187. Fiske, Shirley. "Rules of Address Among Navajo Women in Los Angeles." *Human Organization*. 34 (1978): 72-91.
    A linguistic approach to adaptation and change studies—focuses in a very effective way on network maintenance among urban women.
188. Flannery, Regina. "The Position of Women Among the Eastern Cree." *Primitive Man*. 8 (1935): 81-86.
    A status study—early—from Canada and the Cree—not much depth.
189. ———. "The Position of Women Among the Mescalero Apache." *Primitive Man*. 5 (1932): 26-32.
    Another of Flannery's early status articles based on little but a cursory examination of surface features of the Apachean cultures.
190. Fleming, E. McClung. "The American Image As Indian Princess, 1765-83." *Winterthur Portfolio*. 2 (1968): 65-81.
    An article detailing the various artistic images—Queen and Princess—used by Old World artists and cartographers to portray the delights and hazards of the New World.
191. Forbes, Jack (Powhatan). *Nevada Indians Speak*. Reno: University of Nevada Press, 1967.
    Much on Sarah Winnemucca, though not on other women.
192. Foreman, Carolyn Thomas (Cherokee). "Augusta Robertson Moore: A Sketch of Her Life and Times." *Chronicles Of Oklahoma*. 13 (1935): 399-420.
    One in a series by Foreman on distinguished Indian women of Oklahoma from earlier days—useful and interesting.
193. ———. "Aunt Eliza of Tahlequah." *Chronicles Of Oklahoma*. 9 (1931): 43-55.
    A short biography of Eliza Missouri Bushyhead, one of the early Oklahoma matriarchs from a prominent missionary family.

194. ———. "A Cherokee Pioneer: Ella Flora Coodey Robinson." *Chronicles Of Oklahoma.* 7 (1979): 364-74.

A short biographical sketch of a mid-19th century Cherokee community leader and educator.

195. ———. "A Creek Pioneer: 'Aunt Sue' Rogers and Her Family." *Chronicles Of Oklahoma.* 21 (1943): 271-79.

One of Foreman's series on early Indian women in Oklahoma—this one primarily a McIntosh geneology—as well as about a prominent educator.

196. ———. *Indian Women Chiefs.* Muskogee, Oklahoma: Hoffman, 1954; rep., 1976.

A collage of badly-documented sources on very interesting women and important people—a mine for further research.

197. ———. "Two Notable Women of the Creek Nation." *Chronicles Of Oklahoma.* 35 (Autumn, 1957): 315-37.

Short biographies on Mary Lewis Herrod and Kate Shawahrens, well-known educators in the Creek Nation.

198. Foster, Anna. *The Mohawk Princess: Being Some Account Of The Life Of Tekahionwake (E. Pauline Johnson)* Vancouver: Lion's Gate, 1931.

One of the several romanticized tales of the Canadian Mohawk poet and actress who revitalized cultural attentions to the Mohawk people.

199. Fowler, Catherine S. "Sarah Winnemucca (Hopkins), Northern Paiute." In Margot Liberty, ed. *American Indian Intellectuals.* St. Paul, Minnesota: West Publishing Co., 1978.

A very helpful, detailed account of the available material on this important figure—a demonstration of intellectual leadership.

200. Fox, Nancy. "Rose Gonzales." *American Indian Art Magazine.* (Autumn, 1977): 52-57.

A fairly uninspired article on this fine revivalist potter from San Ildefonso.

201. Fox, Velda Mae. "The Development of the Pocahontas Story in American Literature, 1607-1927." Thesis, University of Iowa, 1927.

One of the many master's thesis and article treatments of the essential American myth in literature.

202. Frazier, Neta Lohnea. *Sacajawea: The Girl Nobody Knows*. New York: David McKay Co.,1967.

    A mundane and fictionalized children's biography of the Shoshone guide.

203. Freeman, Milton. "Social and Ecologic Analysis of Systematic Female Infanticide Among the Netsilek Eskimo." *American Anthropologist*. 73, no. 5 (1971): 1011-18.

    One of several not very persuasive attempts to suggest an environmental basis for female infanticide.

204. Frisbie, Charlotte J. *Kinaalda: A Study Of The Navajo Girls' Puberty Ceremony*. Middletown, Connecticut: Wesleyan University Press, 1967.

    One of several decent modern anthropological examinations of puberty ceremonies, this one more interested in the dramatic performance aspects (narration, song, dance) than in others.

205. ———. *Southwestern Indian Ritual Drama*. Albuquerque, NM: University of New Mexico Press, 1980.

    Apart from a chapter by Farrar on puberty ceremonies, Frisbie's epilogue deals with the roles of women in Southwestern (mainly Navajo and Pueblo) ritual drama—a provocative essay on a needed area of study.

206. Fry, Alan. *The Revenge Of Annie Charlie*. Garden City, New York: Doubleday and Co., 1973.

    A novel about Indian-White relations and Canada's Indians.

207. Fuller, Iola. *The Loon Feather*. New York: Harcourt, Brace and Company, 1941.

    A romantic novel about Tecumseh's daughter—of no particular interest.

208. Garbarino, Merwyn S. "Seminole Girl." *Trans-Action*. 7, no. 4 (1970): 40-46.

    A "caught-between-two worlds" piece notable only for its appearance in a journal usually uninterested in Indians.

209. Garber, Clark. "Eskimo Infanticide." *Scientific Monthly*. 64 (January, 1947): 98-102.

    An unsuccessful attempt to describe Inuit infanticide and posit an acceptable theory for the practice.

210. Garfield, Viola E. "Change in the Marriage Customs of the Tsimshian." Thesis, University of Washington, 1931.

A brief survey of marriage, divorce, kinship and changing attitudes and practices in the Northwest Coastal tribe.

211. "Gertrude Simmons Bonnin Dies." *Indians At Work.* (March, 1938): 23.

A brief obituary of the Sioux composer, teacher, writer, poltical organizer—one of the founders of pan-Indian movements and organizations in the pre-War period.

212. Giese, Paula. "Free Sarah Bad Heart Bull." *North Country Anvil.* 13 (Oct.-Nov., 1974): 64-71.

An article on Wounded Knee II and some of the leaders—several female—arrested during the struggle between Indians and the FBI.

213. Giffen, Fannie Reed. *Oo-Mah-Ha-Ta-Wa-Tha (Omaha City) With Sketches By Suzette LaFlesche Tibbles.* New York: privately published ms., 1913.

A reformist, romanticist trip west with contributions by LaFlesche, one of the current darlings of the reformist movement.

214. Giffen, Naomi M. *The Roles Of Men And Women In Eskimo Culture.* Chicago: University of Chicago Press, 1930.

The standard study of role differences among the Inuit, unusual for its interest and detail in its time—helpful for an articulation of mutuality in roles and status.

215. Gilmore, Anne. "Indian Health Care; What the Dispute Is All About." *Canadian Medical Association Journal.* (July, 1979): 87-94.

One of the many articles about the unnecessary sterilization of American Indian women.

216. Gilmore, M.R. "Notes on the Gynecology and Obstetrics of the Arikara Tribe." *Michigan Academy Of Science Notes And Letters.* 14 (1930): 71-81.

The word "notes" accurately describes this frail and barely informative work.

217. "Girl of the Navajos." 16mm, Color/Sound, 15 minutes, 1977. Produced by Coronet Films.

A very unsophisticated film about traditional Navajo daily life—for children.

218. "God's Drum." 16mm, Color/Sound, 28 minutes, c.1970. Produced and directed by Shawnee Britain for the Univ. of Okla.

A very dramatic, romanticized film starring Te Ata, the popular singer, lecturer and actress—shows pan-Indian "cultural" materials.

219. Goddard, P.E. "Slender Maiden of the Apache." In Elsie Clews Parsons, ed. *American Indian Life*. Lincoln: University of Nebraska Press, 1922; rep. 1967: 147-52.

A personal account of a young Apache woman, rooted in a larger cultural analysis.

220. Gold, Delores. "Psychological Changes Associated With Acculturation of Saskatchewan Indians." *Journal Of Social Work*. 71 (1967): 177-84.

A great deal on women's changing psychology in this general work.

221. Goldenweiser, A. A. "Functions of Women in Iroquois Society." *American Anthropologist*. 17 (1915): 376.

A very brief note on the never-ending debate over Iroquois matriarchy and matriorganization.

222. Goldfrank, Esther S. "Observations on Sexuality Among the Blood Indians of Alberta, Canada." *Psychoanalysis And The Social Sciences*. 3 (1951): 71-98.

"Observations" correctly describes this soft data effort to examine the social manifestations of Blood sexual mores and behavior.

223. Gonzalez, Ellice Becker. "The Changing Economic Roles for MicMac Men and Women: An Ethnohistorical Analysis." Dissertation, State University of New York at Stony Brook, 1979.

A study of the changing roles and statuses of MicMac men and women through time—from a MicMac perspective of change and behavior.

224. Goodpastor, Ed. *LaDonna Harris*. Minneapolis: Dillon Press, 1972.

One of a series of Native biographies for children—many of modern leaders like Harris, who ran for Vice-President of the US in 1980—a decent effort to present Native people for children.

225. Goodwill, Jean Cuthand (Cree). "A New Horizon for Native Women in Canada." In James A. Draper, ed. *Citizen Participation In*

Canada: A Book Of Readings. Toronto: New Press, 1971: 362-370.

A brief documentation of Canadian Native women's new political activism.

226. ———. "Squaw Is A Dirty Word." In Norman Sheffe, ed. *Issues For The Seventies: Canada's Indians.* Toronto: McGraw-Hill, 1970: 50-52.

An attack on stereotyping and a plea for changed behavior.

227. Green, Norma Kidd. "Four Sisters: The Daughters of Joseph LaFlesche." *Nebraska History.* (June, 1964).

A very nice short article on the remarkable sisters, Suzette and Suzanne, and their influential leadership of Indian people and participation in reform movements.

228. ———. *Iron Eyes' Family: The Children Of Joseph LaFlesche.* Lincoln, Nebraska: Johnson Publishing Co., 1969.

A good, thorough, welcome work on this very important and influential Omaha family—Joseph, Francis, Suzette and Suzanne—good to dispel stereotypes about male/female leadership in tribes.

229. Green, Rayna (Cherokee) and Shirley Hill Witt (Mohawk). "Review of *Creek Mary's Blood* and *Shaman's Daughter.*" *Perspectives: A Civil Rights Quarterly.* (Winter, 1981): 38-40; rep. *The Wree-View.* 7 (1982).

Essentially a negative review of *Creek Mary* and a positive one of *Shaman's Daughter*—the review based on an assessment of the historical, cultural and social accuracies therein and their portraits of the women.

230. Green, Rayna (Cherokee). "Honoring the Vision of Changing Woman: A Decade of American Feminism." In Robin Morgan, ed. *Sisterhood Is Global.* New York: Doubleday and Company, forthcoming 1983.

A Native woman's perspective on the last decade of the American women's movement—problems, issues, resolutions.

231. ———. "Diary of A Native American Feminist." *Ms. Magazine.* 10 (July, 1982).

A personal account of the many parts of the American Indian women's movement from the perspective of someone participatory in both Indian and general political action.

232. ———. *Native American Women: A Bibliography.* Wichita Falls, Texas: Ohoyo Resource Center, 1981.

An offprint, less extensive version of 500 annotated items—precursor to the present 700 item library edition.

233. ———. "Native American Women: A Review Essay." *Signs: A Journal Of Women In Culture And Society.* 6, no.2 (Winter, 1980): 248-67.

An extensive review of 300 years of literature, 500 items, on, by, about Native women in America—a critique and guide for remedy of problems.

234. ———. "Native American Women: The Leadership Paradox." *Women's Educational Equity Communications Network News And Notes.* 1, no. 4 (Spring, 1980): 1, 4.

A brief piece on emerging styles of leadership among Native women and organizational efforts to address status problems.

235. ———. "The Pocahontas Perplex: The Image of Indian Women in American Culture." *The Massachussetts Review.* 16, no.4 (1976): 698-714.

A critical survey of the squaw/princess image in American folklore, art, popular culture and literature—and the function of those images.

236. ———. "Review of *Cogewea: The Half-Blood.*" *Tulsa Studies In Women's Literature.* 1, no.2 (1982).

A favorable review of the historic first novel by a Native woman—cites the unique portrait of Indian women in the volume.

237. ———. *That's What She Said: Contemporary Fiction And Poetry By Native American Women.* Bloomington: Indiana University Press, 1983.

An anthology of fiction, poetry, and drama by Native women writers—illustrated by those same women—with an index and introduction and glossary by the editor.

238. Gridley, Marion, comp. *American Indian Women.* New York: Hawthorn Books, 1974.

Popularized, marginally informative biographies of historical and modern women, most taken from Gridley's *Indians Of Today* series.

239. Grinnell, George Bird. "Cheyenne Women's Customs." *American Anthropologist.* 4 (1904).
A collection of miscellaneous behaviors, more interesting from the perspective of the man who was a better artist than anthropologist.

240. ———. "Childbirth Among the Blackfeet." *American Anthropologist.* 9 (1896): 286-87.
The standard early anthropological description of "custom"—this one concerning the practices before, during and after childbirth.

241. Grumet, Robert Severn. "Sunksquaws, Shamans and Tradeswomen: Middle Atlantic Coastal Algonquin Women During the Seventeenth and Eighteenth Centuries." In M. Etienne and E. Leacock, eds. *Women And Colonization.* New York: Praeger, 1980: 43-62.
A fascinating revision of the lives and occupations of little-known women.

242. Guemple, D.L. *Inuit Spouse Exchange.* Chicago: University of Chicago, Dpt. of Anthropology, 1961.
A basic and interesting description of the Inuit custom of spouse exchange, still ignorant, however, of some of its important dimensions.

243. Guillemin, Jeanne. *Urban Renegades: The Cultural Strategy Of American Indians.* New York and London: The Columbia University Press, 1975.
Lots on urban Indian women, their networks and survival tactics for change.

244. Gundlach, James Howard. "The Transition of Native American Indian Fertility." Dissertation, University of Texas at Austin, 1971.
A dissertation describing and examining the changes in the general Native population and its connection with change in fertility.

245. Gundy, H. Pearson. "Molly Brant, Loyalist." *Ontario History.* (Summer, 1953).
Another culturally-biased interpretation of a "helpmeet" figure in Indian-White relations—a misunderstanding of where Brant's— Thayendanaga's sister—loyalties lay.

246. Haas, Mary. "Men's and Women's Speech in Koasati." In Dell Hymes, ed. *Language In Culture And Society.* New York: Harper and Row, 1964: 228-34.

One of the very few works which deals, quite effectively, with male-female speech and different behavioral domains.

247. Hagan, Shirley T. "Descriptive Analysis of Attitudes of Sioux Indian Women Toward Birth Control and Family Planning." Thesis, University of South Dakota, 1971.

Description and very little analysis of Sioux women's attitudes toward family planning.

248. Haile, Father Berard and Karl Luckert, eds. *Women Versus Men: A Conflict Of Navajo Emergence, The Curly To Aheedliinii Version.* Lincoln: University of Nebraska Press, 1981.

An edited presentation of an extended myth narration which shows how men and women separated in Navajo mythology.

249. Hallowell, A. Irving. "Shabwan: A Dissocial Indian Girl." *American Journal Of Orthopsychiatry.* 8, no.2 (1938): 329-40.

A Freudian psychiatric approach, rather orthodox, to a young Native woman perceived as "disturbed." One of the few anthropological analyses of an individual.

250. ———. "Sin, Sex and Sickness in Saulteaux Belief." *British Journal Of Medical Psychology.*" 18 (1939): 191-97.

Devoid of the unecessary Freudian cast to the analysis, this is a fairly straightforward description of what constitutes breaches of good social behavior and what illness might be in sexual terms.

251. Halsell, Grace. *Bessie Yellowhair.* New York: Warner Books, 1974.

A journalist dyes her skin and lives for awhile as a Navajo woman in the Southwest—an exposé of racism best left to Native women.

252. Hamamsy, Laila Shukry. "The Role of Women in a Changing Navajo Society." *American Anthropologist.* 59 (1957): 101-11.

The first article to call attention to significant male-female differences in role and to changes thereof in the important post-World War II period—from a good dissertation (see Shukry).

253. Hammond, Dorothy. "Women: Their Economic Role in Traditional Societies." *A Cummings Module In Anthropology,* 35 (1973).

Quite a bit on Native women in this very conservative, conventional analysis of women's economic roles in traditional societies.

254. "The Hands of Maria." 16mm, Color/Sound, 15 minutes, 1968. Produced by Donald McIntire for Southwest Educational Films.

A short film that shows Maria Martinez making pottery—for schoolchildren.

255. Hanson, Wynne (Sioux). "The Urban Indian Woman and Her Family." *Social Casework: The Journal Of Contemporary Social Work.* (October, 1980): 476-83.

A good summary article on the changes on roles and family life caused by the transition to urban living among many Indian families.

256. Hardacre, Emma. "The Lost Woman of San Nicholas." *Scribner's Monthly.* 20 (September, 1880): 651-64.

One of the first works about the Native recluse of San Nicholas Island—later memorialized in *Island Of The Blue Dolphins.*

257. Harper, E.B. "Fear and the Status of Women." *Southwest Journal Of Anthropology.* 25 (1969): 81-95.

An interesting theoretical article, the thesis of which has been applied to witch persecutions everywhere now, that the level of cultural fear in general is directly related to the status of women— much on Native women.

258. Harris, Marilyn. *Hatter Fox.* New York: Random House,1972.

A truly interesting, but cliched work about a troubled Navajo teenager befriended by a white male social worker—to no avail as usual.

259. Harrisson, Edith. "Women in Navajo Mythology: A Study in the Symbolism of Matriliny." Dissertation, University of Massachussetts, 1973.

A very fine study of the roles and images of women in the mythology surrounding Navajo religious belief and practice.

260. Hart, Donna. "Enlarging the American Dream: Native American Women." *American Education.* 13, no.4 (1977).

A brief summary of statistics on employment and education— interesting in light of their inadequacies as statistics.

261. Hart, Hazel (Chippewa). "Ge Chi Maung Won: The Life Story of an Old Chippewa Woman." In T.D. Allen, ed. *Arrows Four.* Washington: BIA Creative Writing Program, 1972: 31-37.

A life story of a relative by a young girl—one of the first Indian Foxfire-like narratives.

262. Hartley, Lois Neal. "Pocahontas Plays, 1800-1855." Thesis, Pennsylvania State University, 1945.

One of several treatments of the Pocahontas theme in literature—this one on a very popular early genre—drama.

263. Hartman, L.D. "The Life and Customs of the Navajo Woman." *Wisconsin Archaeologist.* XVIII (1938): 100-07.

A very conventional and traditional anthropological article which offers nothing of interest or substance.

264. Hauptman, Lawrence. *The Iroquois And The New Deal.* Syracuse, New York: Syracuse University Press, 1982.

A fine chapter on Alice Lee Jemison and her resistance to John Collier's New Deal—a longer effort from Hauptman's previous work.

265. ———. "Alice Jemison: Seneca Political Activist." *The Indian Historian.* 12, no. 2 (1974): 15-40.

A very welcome and thorough revisionist analysis of the literature on Alice Lee Jemison—defining her as a nationalist rather than as a neo-Nazi slandered by John Collier.

266. Haynes, Terry L. "Some Factors Related to Contraceptive Behavior Among Wind River Shoshone and Arapaho Females." *Human Organization.* 36, no. 1 (1977): 72-76.

Cultural, social, and psychological factors which might contribute to acceptance or rejection of birth control.

267. Healy, William J. "Women of Red River: Being A Book Written From the Recollections of Women Surviving." *Red River Era Centennial Edition.* Minneapolis: Ross and Haines, 1967.

Several minor, but interesting narratives from Native women.

268. Heizer, Robert. *Original Accounts Of The Lone Woman Of San Nicholas Island.* Ramona, Ca.: Ballena Press, 1973.

Oral histories and narratives about Juana Maria, the recluse of San Nicholas Island—good for folklore about Indian women and hermit-like figures.

269. Helm, June. "Female Infanticide, European Diseases: Population Levels Among the McKenzie Dene." *American Ethnologist.* (1980): 259-85.

A fascinating reappraisal of patterns of female infanticide—looks at pressures from disease.

270. Herold, Joyce. "The Basketry of Tanzanita Pesata." *American Indian Art Magazine*. (Spring, 1978): 26-29, 94.

A brief work detailing something of the life and work of the traditional basketmaker—a good look at her innovations in traditional design.

271. Hewitt, J.N.B. "Status of Women in Iroquois Polity Before 1784." *Smithsonian Annual Report For 1932*. Washington, DC: Government Printing Office, 1933: 475-88.

One of the first of the many articles on Iroquois matriarchy and female status to call attention to the vast changes in that status after 1760.

272. Hilger, M. Inez. "Arapaho Child Life and Its Cultural Background." *Bureau Of American Ethnology Bulletin*. 148 (1952).

Mostly random notes on child rearing, though a great deal of material on maternal behavior when surrogate parent—grandmother and aunt—behavior should have been documented.

273. ———. "Chippewa Food and Pre-Natal Conduct Taboos." *Primitive Man*. 9 (1936): 46-48.

A meaningless, non-contextual list of curiosities.

274. Hilger, Sister Mary Ione. *The First Sioux Nun: Sister Marie-Josephine Nebraska, SGM, 1859-94*. Milwaukee, Wisconsin: Bruce Publishing Co., 1963.

A semi-fictional account of the first Sioux nun by an anthropologist who worked among the Sioux.

275. Hill, Florence Smith (Mohawk). "Patriotic Work of the Six Nations Women in World Wars I and II." In Six Nations Agricultural Society,ed. *Six Nations Indians Yesterday and Today, 1867-1942*. Onandaga, New York: Six Nations Agricultural Society, 1942: 52-53.

A too brief account of Iroquois women's activities in wartime.

276. Hill, W. W. "Note on the Pima Berdache." *American Anthropologist*. 40 (1938): 338-40.

One of two pieces by Hill on sexuality and sexual behavior among Southwest tribes; interesting because it comments on female transsexual behavior as well as on that of males.

277. ———. "The Status of the Hermaphrodite and Transvestite in Navajo Culture." *American Anthropologist*. 37 (1935): 273-79.

Another of Hill's works, quite brief, on transsexual and homo-
sexual behavior among Southwestern tribes—does comment on
such behavior among women.
278. Himes, Norman E. "The Practice of Contraception and Its Relation
to Some Phases of Population Theory." Dissertation, Harvard
University, 1939.
Surveys many methods supposedly employed by Native peoples
to effect contraception.
279. Hippler, Arthur E. "Additional Perspective on Eskimo Female Infanticide." *American Anthropologist.* 74 (1972): 1318-19.
A very brief and putatively explanatory note on the controversial
practice of female infanticide.
280. Hiwalking, Belle (Cheyenne) with Katherine M. Weist, ed. *Belle
Hiwalking: The Narrative Of A Northern Cheyenne Woman.* Bill-
ings: Montana Council for Indian Education, 1979.
A new style of autobiography, commissioned by Indians for an
Indian audience—by a woman who has seen many changes in her
tribe—very worthwhile reading.
281. Hodge, Frederick Webb. "Sacajawea." *Handbook Of American Indians North Of Mexico,* V.II. Washington, DC: Government
Printing Office, 1910.
A brief biographical sketch of little use.
282. Hodge, Zahrah P. "Maria Martinez, Indian Master Potter." *Southern Workman.* 62, no. 5 (1933).
One of the very few articles on Indians in this liberal journal from
the South—this on the increasingly known potter from San Ildefonso.
283. Hoebel, Edward Adamson. "Eskimo Infanticide and Polyandry."
Scientific Monthly. (June, 1947).
One of the many attempts to find explanations for the practice of
female infanticide—this based in polyandry.
284. Hoffman, W. J. "The Midewiwin or 'Grand Medicine Society' of
the Ojibwa." *Bureau Of American Ethnology Director's Report,
1885-86.* Washington, DC: Government Printing Office, 1891.
A very early source documenting the level and type of female
participation in healing and ceremonial behavior of an institutionalized type.

285. Hogan, Linda (Chickasaw), ed. *Frontiers:* Special Issue on Native American Women. 6, no. 2 (1982).

    A special issue of a noted women's studies journal including essays, poems, fiction, oral histories, analysis of issues—by Native and non-Native authors.

286. Honigmann, Irma and John. "Child-Rearing Patterns Among the Great Whale Eskimo." *Anthropological Papers Of The University Of Alaska.* 2 (1952): 31-50.

    A decent descriptive piece on male and female differential behavior in child-rearing.

287. "Hopi Indians." Super 8, Color/Silent, c. 1970. Produced and distributed by Ealing.

    Parts of the series—filmed by Hopi—show women making piki bread, baskets, rugs and pottery.

288. Hopkins, Sarah Winnemucca (Paiute). *Life Among The Paiutes: Their Wrongs And Claims.* Boston: Putnam, 1883; rep. *Old West.* 2 (Fall, 1965): 49-96.

    The classic political autobiography—details Winnemucca's life and growing political consciousness as well as the Paiute case—by a complex, controversial woman.

289. Hostbjor, Stella. "Social Services to the Indian Unmarried Mother." *Child Welfare Magazine.* 41 (1961): 7-9.

    A typical social welfare piece describing the kinds of social services to women defined by non-Indians as unmarried women with il-ligitimate children.

290. Howard, Harold P. *Sacajawea.* Norman: University of Oklahoma Press, 1971.

    One of several "standard" works on the Bird Woman—takes a fairly conventional, but authoritative approach to her history.

291. Howard, Helen. "The Mystery of Sacajawea's Death." *Pacific Northwest Quarterly.* (January, 1967).

    One of several speculative articles on Sacajawea, her time and place of birth—not especially helpful.

292. Howell, Elmo. "The Chickasaw Woman: William Faulkner's Story." *Chronicles Of Oklahoma.* 49, no.3 (1971): 334-39.

    A brief look at Faulkner's story of the Chickasaw woman as it reveals Faulkner's knowledge of the Mississippi Chickasaws and his use of them and the woman as metaphor for part of the Southern racial experience.

293. Hubbell, Jay B. "The Smith-Pocahontas Story in Literature." *Virginia Magazine Of History And Biography*. (July, 1957).

A descriptive survey of the American literary obsession with Captain Smith and the Native princess—good for the variety and historical span of the works covered.

294. Hudson, Travis. "An Additional Note on the 'Lone Woman' of San Nicholas." *Masterkey*. 52 (1978): 151-54.

More on the hermit-like Juana Maria who inspired *"Island Of The Blue Dolphins"*.

295. Hultkrantz, Akė. *The Religion Of The American Indians*. Berkeley: University of California, 1978: 41, 47, 53, 55, 112, 136, 117, 161, 114, 115, 149, 275.

The little and insignificant material on women indicates the vast scholarly ignorance of their behavior in this major work.

296. Hungry Wolf, Beverley (Blood/Blackfeet). *The Ways Of My Grandmothers*. New York: William Morrow and Co., 1981.

A fascinating collage of autobiographical material, bits of information about traditional ways, and personal statements from this educated woman very attuned to traditional ways.

297. Hunt, JoJo (Lumbee). "American Indian Women and Their Relationship to the Federal Government." In Dpt. of Ed./ Nat'l. Inst. of Ed. *Conference On The Educational and Occupational Needs Of American Indian Women, 1976*. Washington, DC: GPO, 1980: 293-312.

An account of the impacts of federal policy on Native women's status.

298. Hurt, Wesley R. and Richard M. Brown. "Social Drinking Patterns of the Yankton Sioux." *Human Organization*. 24 (1965): 222-30.

An analysis of Sioux social drinking, with much on male-female differences.

299. Huyghe, Patrick and David Konigsberg. "Bury My Heart At New York City." *New York*. (February 26, 1979): 53-57.

A great deal of material on urban Native women and their coping strategies for stress and change in the city.

300. "I Know Who I Am." B and W videotape, 30 minutes. Written and produced by Sandra Osawa (Makah) for Upstream Productions. A film made to show the importance of family life and family retention—interviews with women community leaders from the Northwest Coast tribes.

301. Icolari, Dan, ed. *Reference Book Of The American Indian: Who's Who.* Rye, New York: Todd Publishers, 1974.

Brief biographies and lists of accomplishments of Indian and non-Indian men and women—hastily and unprofessionally assembled for a quick-profit volume—not too helpful.

302. Indian Rights Association. *Indian Truth: Special Issue on Native Women.* 239 (May-June, 1981).

Notes on current national and community leaders, on issues that affect Native women, on women's organizations—focus on Rayna Green's scholarly work on Native women and an interview with Janet McCloud about activism.

303. International Indian Treaty Council. *Native American Women.* New York: United Nations, 1975.

A political tract stating political concerns of Native people including statements on land claims, political persecution, status.

304. Irwin, Hadley. *We Are Mesquakie, We Are One.* Old Westbury, New York: Feminist Press, 1980.

A children's novel dealing with the life of a Mesquakie (Fox) girl and her tribe's struggle to survive—some cliches but decent nevertheless.

305. "Island of the Blue Dolphins." 16mm, Color/Sound, 20 minutes, 1966. Produced by Robert Radnitz for Teaching Film Custodians, Inc.

A film of Scott O'Dell's well-known novel about Juana Maria, the hermit-like exile of a California coastal island.

306. Jackson, Helen Hunt. *Ramona.* Boston: Roberts Brothers, 1884.

The essential romantic novel—famous as the Indian "Uncle Tom's Cabin," by a reformer and Indian rights advocate who wanted to and did start the Indian reform movements of the early 20th century.

307. Jacobs, Melville, ed. *Clackamas Chinook Texts. 2 Vols.* Bloomington, Indiana: Indiana Resource Center in Anthropology, Folklore and Linguistics, 1958.

This work features the narrations of traditional Clackamas Chinook tales by Victoria Howard.

308. Jacobs, Sue-Ellen. "Berdache: A Brief Review of the Literature." *Colorado Anthropology.* 1 (1977): 25-40.

A very fine and critical review of the literature on berdache which is both biased about male behavior and neglectful of the female tradition.

309. ———. "Continuity and Change in Gender Roles at San Juan Pueblo, New Mexico." In Alfonso Ortiz, ed. *Changes In The Tewa World.* Albuquerque: University of New Mexico Press, 1982.

An examination through time—very fine—of the sex-role identity patterns in a Pueblo group.

310. ———. *Women In Perspective: A Guide For Cross-Cultural Studies.* Chicago: University of Illinois Press, 1976.

The subtitle is quite descriptive of this useful work which lists extensive bibliographic notes to the ethnographic literature on Native and other women—all phases of human behavior.

311. Jahner, Elaine. "The Novel and Oral Tradition: An Interview With Leslie Marmon Silko." *Book Forum: American Indians Today.* 3 (1981): 383-99.

An interview with Silko about the connections between her work and oral tradition—particularly Puebloan traditions.

312. James, Edward T., ed. *Notable American Women,* 3 Vols. Cambridge: Harvard University Press, 1971.

Authoritative treatments of Gertrude Bonnin, Molly Brant, Alice Brown Davis, Marie Dorion, Milly Francis, Mary Musgrove, the LaFlesche sisters, Pocahontas, Sacajawea, Kateri Tekakwitha, Roberta Lawson, etc.

313. Jeffrey, Julie Roy. *Frontier Women: The Trans-Mississippi West, 1840-1880.* Boston: Hill and Wang, 1981.

A very fine book on the role of women in the trans-Mississippi West—some on interactions between Indian and white women.

314. Jenkins, William Warren. "Three Centuries of the Pocahontas Story in Literature." Dissertation, University of Tennessee, 1977.

     A comprehensive survey of the quintessential American myth in literature—one in a series of such treatments.

315. Johnson, Emily Pauline (Mohawk). *The Moccassin Maker.* Toronto: Ryerson, 1913.

     The autobiography of the Mohawk poet, actress and cultural leader, including a nice biography of her mother—good for comparison to other biographies of her.

316. Johnson, Evelyn H.C. (Mohawk). "Grandfather and Father of E. Pauline Johnson." *Archaeological Reports,* the Ministry of Education in Ontario (1928): 44-47.

     A focus on the distinguished male predecessors of the poet and actress so well-known in her time.

317. Johnson, Lusita G. and Stephen Proskauer. "Hysterical Psychosis in a Prepubescent Navajo Girl." *Journal Of The American Academy Of Child Psychiatry.* 13 (Winter, 1974): 1-119.

     The very long study of the diagnosis and treatment, from an orthodox perspective, of a psychotic adolescent.

318. Johnston, Jean. "Molly Brant: Mohawk Matron." *Ontario History.* 56 (June, 1964): 105-24.

     One of the very few works on Molly Brant, the common law wife of Sir William Johnston, the Crown administrator of Mohawk country and the essential broker between the British and the Mohawks.

319. Jones, David. *Sanapia: A Comanche Medicine Woman.* New York: Holt, Rinehart and Winston, 1968.

     Recommended for the focus on the life of a medicine woman, but acknowledged for failures to see Sanapia as more than a "cultural" leader.

320. Jones, Louis Thomas. "Eloquent Indian Women." *Aboriginal American Oratory.* Los Angeles: Southwest Museum, 1965: 113-20.

     Examples of speaking from well-known Native women like Gertrude Simmons Bonnin—a welcome departure from the eloquent chief tradition.

321. Jordan, B. Kathryn. "Discerning Real and Ideal Perceptions of Women in Michoacan and Montana." Dissertation, University of Oregon, 1978.
An examination of the folklore, mythology, and popular percepions and images of women in a Mexican and Montana Indian community—separating real treatment and perception from the idealized.
322. Joskowski, Helen. "My Heart Will Go Out: Healing Songs of Native American Women." *International Journal Of Women's Studies.* 4, no.2 (1981): 118-34.
Contrasts the difference in text translation form, of Native women's healing songs with men's—does not make tribal and cultural distinctions clear.
323. Katz, Jane B. *This Song Remembers: Self-Portraits Of Native Americans In The Arts.* Boston: Houghton-Mifflin, 1980.
A book which includes personal narratives and biographical sketches of modern Native women artists like Grace Medicine Flower, Helen Hardin, Mary Morez Pitseolak.
324. Katz, Jane B., ed. *I Am The Fire Of Time.* Boston: EP Dutton, 1977.
A miscellaneous collection of poems, oral narratives, personal accounts, statements which offers very little of substance or clarity.
325. Kayser, David W. "A Navajo Julia Child." *El Palacio.* 77, no. 2 (19971): 37-40.
An article on a Navajo traditional cook who promotes old-style foods and methods to Navajo and non-Navajo people.
326. Kegg, Maude (Ojibwa) with John Nichols, ed. *Gu-lkwezenswiyaan, When I Was A Little Girl.* Onamia, Michigan; privately printed, 1976.
An Ojibwa/English memoir from a woman who describes family life and traditional activities at the turn of the century.
327. Kegg, Maude (Ojibwa). "Gabekanaansiy, At the End of the Trail: Memories of Chippewa Childhood in Minnesota." *Occasional Publications In Anthropology:* University of North Carolina Museum of Anthropology Linguistic Series. 4 (1978).
An English/Ojibwa description of traditional life early in the century.

328. Kehoe, Alice B. "The Function of Ceremonial Sexual Intercourse Among the Northern Plains Indians." *Plains Anthropologist.* 15, no. 48 (1970): 99-103.

A brief article on ritual sexual intercourse between persons of power or those seeking to gain it.

329. ———. "Old Woman Had Great Power." *Western Canadian Journal Of Anthropology.* 6, no.3 (1976): 68-76.

Examines the two areas, sacred and secular, in which Blackfeet women can have power—defined as strength and autonomy in Blackfeet terms—a woman who has distinguished herself has access to ritual and social power.

330. Keith, Anne. "The Navajo Girl's Puberty Ceremony: Function and Meaning For the Adolescent." *El Palacio.* 71, no.1 (1964): 27-36.

Some attempt to interpret, through the adolescents experiencing it, the role and meaning of the kinaalda, or puberty ceremony.

331. Kelley, Jane Holden. *Yaqui Women: Contemporary Life Histories.* Lincoln: University of Nebraska Press, 1977.

A fine volume, recommended for its treatment of ordinary Yaqui women's lives—and for the author's honesty about her own methodology and the effect of her presence. Especially good for an appreciation of the effects of removal.

332. Kent, Susan. "Hogans, Sacred Circles and Symbols: The Navajo Use of Space." In David Brugge and Charlotte J. Frisbie, eds. *Essays In Honor Of Leland Wyman.* Santa Fe: Museum of New Mexico Press, 1982.

A fine article that has much on female real and symbolic use of space.

333. ———. "The Use and Refuse of Activity Areas: An Ethnoarchaeological Study of Spatial Patterning." Dissertation, University of New Mexico, 1981.

A dissertation which pays heavy attention to male-female differences in the use of space in the Southwest, with particular reference to Navajo.

334. Keshena, Rita (Menominee). "Relevancy of Tribal Interests and Tribal Diversity in Determining Educational Needs of American Indians." In Dpt. of Ed./Nat'l. Inst. of Ed. *Conference On The*

Educational And Occupational Needs Of American Indian Women,
1976. Washington, DC: GPO, 1980: 231-51.
More about the tribal factor in Indian development than about
women.

335. Khattah, Hind Abou Seoud. "Current Roles of Ramah Navajo
Women and Their Natality Behavior." Dissertation, University
of North Carolina at Chapel Hill, 1974.
A very conventional anthropological study of maternal behavior—
nothing new to offer.

336. Kidwell, Clara Sue (Chippewa-Choctaw). "American Indian Women:
Problems of Communicating a Cultural/Sexual Identity." *The
Creative Woman.* 2, no.3 (1979): 33-38.
Touches on the difficulties of maintaining Indian identity and
appropriate gender role and conveying that in a non-Indian setting.

337. ———. "The Power of Women in Three American Indian Societies." *Journal Of Ethnic Studies.* 6, no.3 (1979): 113-21.
A brief review of the traditional paths to and definitions of female
power and status in three traditional Native societies.

338. ———. "Review of Bright Eyes: The Story Of Suzette LaFlesche,
An Omaha Indian." *Journal Of Ethnic Studies.* 2 (Winter, 1975):
119-22.
A critical and substantive review showing the popularized nature
of the book and its treatment of LaFlesche.

339. ———. "The Status of American Indian Women in Higher Education." In Dpt. of Ed./Nat'l. Inst. of Ed. *Conference On The
Educational And Occupational Needs Of American Indian Women,
1976.* Washington, DC: GPO, 1980: 83-123.
An assessment of problems and needs taken from bad statistics.

340. Kilpatrick, Jack and Anna (Cherokee). *Friends Of Thunder: Folktales Of The Oklahoma Cherokees.* Dallas, Texas: Southern Methodist University Press, 1964.
Dadayi, Gahno, Gatey, Tsiwon and other female narrators in this
fine book in a series of works on Cherokee folklore.

341. Kilpatrick, Jack F. (Cherokee), ed. "From the Narratives of Lucy
Lowry Hoyt Keys (Waknenauki)." Bureau of American Ethnology Anthropology Papers 73. 196 (1966): 175-213.

An intriguing edition of the letters and diaries of an upper-class, well-educated woman of the planter-class Cherokee in North Carolina. Interesting for her view of well-known male Cherokee figures.

342. Kimball, Yeffe (Osage) with Jean Anderson. *The Art Of American Indian Cooking*. New York: Doubleday and Co., 1965.

A good solid introduction to the culinary arts of many tribes—not always the most traditional recipes, many adapted for American kitchens.

343. King, E. Sterling. *The Wild Rose Of The Cherokee, Nancy Ward, The Pocahontas Of The West*. privately printed, 1895.

One of the initial, romanticized, nearly fictional account of this major leader, the Beloved Woman of the tribe.

344. Kingston, C.S. "Sacajawea As Guide." *Pacific Northwest Quarterly*. 35 (January, 1944): 3.

A brief look at Sacajawea's putative competence as a guide—concludes she was competent.

345. Kirgis, Carol Ann. "A Study of Health Care and Health Education for Navajo Pregnant Women." Dissertation, University of Utah, 1978.

An examination of the kinds of programs for pre-natal care that exist for on-reservation Navajo women.

346. Kjellstrom, Rolf. *Eskimo Marriage*. Lund, Norway: Berlingsha Boktryckeriet, 1973.

A description of the various forms and understanding of marriage among the Inuit.

347. Klagetoh Maiden Singers. "The Klagetoh Maiden Singers." LP Recording from Indian House Records, c. 1975.

Well-known traditional Navajo women singers sing skip, round, spin, and 2-step songs—very fine.

348. Klein, Laura F. " 'She's One of Us, You Know.': The Public Life of Tlingit Women: Tradition, History and Contemporary Perspectives." *Western Canadian Journal Of Anthropology*. 6, no.3 (1976): 164-83.

Discusses the sexually egalitarian nature of public leadership in modern and historical Tlingit society.

349. ———. "Tlingit Women and Town Politics." Dissertation, New York University, 1975.

The earlier, longer, more detailed version of Klein's very interesting work on the roles of Tlingit women in the new political order of Alaskan politics and tribal government.

350. ———. "Contending With Colonization: Tlingit Men and Women in Change." In Mona Etienne and Eleanor Leacock, eds. *Women And Colonization: Anthropological Perspectives.* New York: Praeger Books, 1980.

Another of Klein's fine works on Tlingit women and cultural change.

351. Kluckhohn, Clyde. "Navajo Women's Knowledge of Their Song Ceremonials." In Richard Kluckhohn, ed. *Culture And Behavior.* New York: The Free Press, 1962: 92-96.

A short and very interesting piece on women's participation in and knowledge of primarily male domains of behavior.

352. Knudsen, R.R. *Fox Running.* New York: Avon, 1975.

A very nice novel for young people about an Apache girl—a competitive runner in a predominantly white world—especially good for the portrayal of the very live traditional and new interest in women running.

353. Krech, Shepard. "Matriorganization: The Basis of Aboriginal Subarctic Social Organization." *Arctic Anthropology.* (Winter, 1981).

An article interesting only for its treatment of a group not unusually examined for its "matriorganization."

354. Krepps, Ethel (Kiowa-Miami). "Equality in Education for Indian Women." *Indian Historian.* 13, no. 2 (1980): 9.

A lawyer's view of the growing educational achievements of Native women and the problems remaining to that achievement.

355. Kroeber, Alfred L. "Ethnology of the Gros Ventre." *American Museum Of Natural History Bulletin.* I, no.4 (1908): 216-21. rep. 1978.

The short story of the capture and eventual escape of Watches-All, a Gros Ventre woman, from the Blackfeet.

356. ———. "Handbook of the Indians of California." *Bureau Of American Ethnology Bulletin.* 78 (1925): 63-66.

An unusual account of the growth and initiation of a Yurok medicine woman—a religious leader and healer.

357. Kumagai, Gloria L., ed. *American Women Of Color: Integrating Cultural-Diversity Into Non-Sex-Biased Curriculum.* St. Paul, MN. Pub. Schools, 1982.

Some curricular materials (teacher training guides, bibliography, filmstrips) on American Indian women, other groups for teachers.

358. Kunitz, Stephen J. "Navajo and Hopi Fertility, 1971-72." *Human Biology.* 46, no. 3 (1974): 435-51.

A comparative study of pregnancy and birth rates between the two tribes.

359. ———. "The Relation of Economic Variations to Mortality and Fertility Patterns on the Navajo Reservation." *Lake Powell Research Project Bulletin.* no. 20 (1976).

A very helpful study examining the relationships, work, food supply, and work behavior to the death and fertility rates on the Navajo.

360. ———. "A Survey Of Fertility History and Contraceptive Use Among a Group Of Navajo." *Lake Powell Research Project Bulletin.* no. 21 (1976).

An attempt to determine certain of the factors that in turn determine population and population change.

361. Kunitz, Stephen J. and John C. Slocumb. "The Changing Sex Ratio of the Navajo Tribe." *Social Biology.* 23 (1976).

One of several articles on population among the Navajo by this research team—useful as indicators of change.

362. ———. "The Use of Surgery to Avoid Childbearing Among Navajo and Hopi Indians." *Human Biology.* (February, 1976): 18.

A description of a survey done to determine the reasons among Hopi and Navajo for requesting surgical sterilization.

363. Kurath, Gertrude P. "Matriarchal Dances of the Iroquois." In Sol Tax, ed. *Indian Tribes Of Aboriginal America.* Chicago: University of Chicago Press, 1952.

A brief exploration of the "women's dance" or dances of the Iroquois—their role and meaning in Iroquoian art and life.

364. Kuttner, Robert E. and Albert B. Lorincz. "Promiscuity and Prostitution in Urbanized Indian Communities." *Mental Hygeine.* 54, no. 1 (1970): 79-91.

A classic social welfare treatment of behavior in an urban community—Western definitions for non-Western behaviors.

365. LaFlesche, Francis (Omaha). "Osage Marriage Customs." *American Anthropologist.* 14 (1912): 127-30.

A short, straightforward descriptive piece from one of the first Western-trained Indian anthropologists—one of the well-known and influential LaFlesche family.

366. Lake, Robert G. "Chilula Religion and Ideology: A Discussion of Native American Humanistic Concepts and Processes." *Humboldt Journal Of Social Relations.* 7, no. 2 (1980): 113-34.

A discussion of religion and ideology among the Chilula Indians of California—particularly concerned with the role and function of women.

367. Lamphere, Louise. *To Run After Them: The Cultural And Social Bases Of Cooperation In A Navajo Community.* Tucson: University of Arizona Press, 1977.

Much discussion of the roles and status of women in this community study—an entire chapter on strategies in cooperation/conflict among women.

368. Lampman, E.S. *Navajo Sister.* Garden City, New York: Doubleday and Co., 1956.

A rather banal story—for children—about a Navajo girl.

369. Landes, Ruth. *The Ojibwa Religion And The Midewiwin.* Madison: University of Wisconsin Press, 1968.

The standard work on Ojibwa religion, complete with extensive references to the roles of women in the grand medicine society.

370. ———. *The Ojibwa Woman.* New York: W.W. Norton and Co., 1971.

One of the first book-length works on Native women, an essential classic, however flawed by its real and profound bias toward the importance of male behavior.

371. Lantis, Margaret. *Eskimo Childhood And Interpersonal Relationships: Biographies With Geneologies.* Seattle: University of Washington Press, 1960.

An unusual comparative biographical approach, with a number of women's narratives, to a customary area of study in anthropology.

372. Lavallee, Mary Ann (Cree). "Problems That Concern Indian Women: A Report From the Saskatchewan Indian Women's Conference." *Qu'Appelle.* (November 7, 1967): 10-15.

A popular account discussing attempts of Canadian Native women to change their discriminatory status under the Indian Acts.

373. ———. "Yesterday's Indian Women: The Role of Native Women, Past, Present, Future." *Tawow.* 1 (Spring, 1970): 7.

A very short, but strong statement about the historical roles of Native women from Canada—revised from a conference speech (see Alberta Native Women's Society).

374. Leacock, Eleanor and Jacqueline Goodman. "Montagnais Marriage and the Jesuits in the 17th Century: Incidents From the Relations of Paul LeJeune." *Western Canadian Journal Of Anthropology.* 6, no.3 (1976): 77-91.

A fascinating work looking at the Jesuit insistence on obedience to authority and the impact of that insistence on the status of Native women.

375. Leacock, Eleanor B. "Matrilocality in a Simple Hunting Economy (Montagnais Naskapi)." *Southwest Journal Of Anthropology.*" 11 (Spring, 1955): 31-47.

An insightful and thorough work about the participation and influence of women in a hunting economy—predates new feminist revisionist theory on such behaviors.

376. ———. "Review of Spindler's Menominee Women." *American Anthropologist.* 65, no. 4 (1963): 940-42.

A good critical piece on the blessings and defects of an influential piece of work—especially good for its brief comments on the methodology for work with tribal women.

377. Lee, Bobbie (Metis). *Bobbie Lee, Indian Rebel: Struggles Of A Native Canadian Woman.* Richmond, B.C.: LSM Press, 1975.

An utterly compelling and unusual autobiography of a young, urban Metis woman—of her life on drugs and alcohol and her eventual activism in radical Indian politics of the seventies.

378. Lee, Dorothy Demetracopoulou. "A Wintu Girl's Puberty Ceremony." *New Mexico Anthropology.* 4, no. 4 (1940): 57-60.
     A brief description of puberty ceremonies, interesting primarily because it is not of the much-studied Apache or Navajo.
379. Leevier, Mrs. Annette (Ojibwa). *The Psychic Experiences Of An American Indian Princess.* Los Angeles: Austin Publishing Company, 1920.
     The story of a woman's life as a psychic and Christian faith healer—part show business, part autobiography.
380. Lewis, Ann (Mohawk-Delaware). "Separate Yet Sharing." *The Conservationist.* 30 (January-February, 1976): 17.
     Discusses mutuality and interdependence between Native men and women in an agrarian society.
381. Lewis, Claudia. *Indian Families Of The Northwest Coast: Impact Of Change.* Chicago: University of Chicago Press, 1971.
     An essential work on culture change studies, particularly notable for its focus on both males and females.
382. Lewis, Oscar. "Manly-Hearted Women Among the North Piegan." *American Anthropologist.* 43 (1941): 173-87.
     One of the first articulations about aggressive and war-like behavior, honored by the tribe, among women—an over-dramatized but useful piece.
383. Linderman, Frank, editor. *Pretty Shield, A Crow Medicine Woman (Red Mother).* New York: John Day and Co., 1932; rep. 1974.
     The very much edited and retouched narrative of a Crow Medicine woman—good for descriptions of traditional female roles and the changes wrought by contact.
384. Lindsey, Lilah Denton. "Memories of the Indian Territory Mission Field." *Chronicles Of Oklahoma.* 36 (Summer, 1958): 181-98.
     A predictable, if welcome missionary piece which offers "memories" of a number of Native women—some good anecdotal material.
385. *Listening Post,* A Periodical of the Mental Health Program-Indian Health Service, Albuquerque: Special Issue on Indian Women. 4, no.2 (1982).
     An entire issue for Indian Health Service employees on Indian women—rural and urban, traditional and changing—most by Na-

tive women and focusing on collective and individual strengths for endurance and change.

386. Livingston, Katherine Sheila. "Contemporary Iroquois Women and Work: A Study of Consciousness of Inequality." Dissertation, Cornell University, 1974.

A useful and interesting work on the changing roles of Iroquois women in work and their knowledge and articulation of their unequal status in the eyes of prospective employers and their own male relatives.

387. Loeb, Catherine. "La Chicana: A Bibliographic Survey." *Frontiers.* 5, no.2 (1981).

A good bibliographic survey and analysis of the literature on Chicanas in the US—relevant to Indian women in terms of rural Chicanas and those of an Indian background.

388. Lone Dog, Louise (Mohawk-Delaware). *Strange Journey: The Vision Quest Of A Psychic Indian Woman.* Healdsburg, California: Naturegraph Press, 1964.

A book for modern non-Indian cult markets, with emphasis on non-Native psychic experiences—worthwhile only for its insights into marginal people.

389. Longboat, Mary Anderson (Mohawk). "Emily Pauline Johnson." In Six Nations Agricultural Society, ed. *Six Nations Yesterday And Today, 1942-67.* Onandaga, New York: Six Nations Agricultural Society, 1967.

A short memorial piece about the important poet and leader.

390. Lowie, Robert H. "A Crow Woman's Tale." In Elsie Clews Parsons. *American Indian Life.* Lincoln: University of Nebraska Press, 1967: 35-40.

One of the many autobiographical narratives, taken down to "reveal the culture" of a particular "informant."

391. Lubart, Joseph M. "Field Study of the Problems of Adaptation of MacKenzie Delta Eskimos to Social and Economic Change." *Psychiatry.* 32 (1967): 447-58.

A discussion primarily of the negative aspects of change, focused on both males and females.

392. Lurie, Nancy O. "Indian Women: A Legacy of Freedom." *Look To The Mountaintop*. San Jose, Ca.: Gousha Publications, 1972:29-36.

An interesting examination, though brief, of the various kinds of personal and traditional autonomy enjoyed by Native women.

393. ———. *Mountain-Wolf Woman, Sister Of Crashing Thunder, A Winnebago Indian*. Ann Arbor: University of Michigan Press, 1961.

The classic and still fine autobiography of a Native woman—the unintrusive and sensitive editorship as good as the narrative itself.

394. ———. "A Papago Woman and a Woman Anthropologist." *Reviews In Anthropology*. 7 (Winter, 1980), 120.

A fascinating critique by someone who's written a similar book, of Ruth Underhill's autobiographical editing of the life of Maria Chona—sheds much light on the relationship between editor and narrator.

395. Manfred, Frederick. *The Manly-Hearted Woman*. New York: Crown Publishers, 1976.

A powerful and unusual, though gloomy, novel about a warrior woman and leader.

396. Manitowabi, Edna (Ojibwa). *An Indian Girl In The City*. Buffalo, New York: Friends of Malatesta, 1976.

An autobiographical memoir about a young woman's experiences away from the reservation.

397. ———. "An Ojibwa Girl in the City." *This Magazine Is About Schools*. 4 (Fall, 1970): 8-24.

An abstract of a young Indian girl's experience away from reservation life—leads to a full memoir in 1976.

398. Mansfield-Kelley, Diane. "Oliver LaFarge and the Indian Woman in American Literature." Dissertation, University of Texas at Austin, 1979.

A study of the way in which Oliver LaFarge, the novelist and policy-maker, conceived of Native women in his artistic work—shows his romanticization of women and his trivilization of them.

399. Markoosie. "Two Sisters." *North*/Nord. 18, no. 1 (1971): 23-25.

Brief biographical achievement notes on two Canadian Native women of distinction in their communities.

400. Marquis, Thomas, comp. "Iron Teeth, A Cheyenne Old Woman."
     Cheyenne And Sioux. Butte, Montana: privately printed, 1922: 4-
     26.
     A journalistic, romanticized piece by the prolific Marquis—in-
     teresting but hard to trust for validity.
401. Marriott, Alice and Carol Rachlin. *Dance Around The Sun: The
     Life Of Mary Little Bear Inkanish*. New York: T.Y. Crowell,
     1977.
     An unappreciated autobiographical narrative from a fine crafts-
     woman and traditionalist—adds much to the much-studied Chey-
     enne.
402. Marriott, Alice. *Maria Of San Ildefonso*. Norman: University of
     Oklahoma Press, 1946.
     One of the "popular" classics about Maria Martinez and her
     family—a detailed review of her history, her family's work, and
     her development of the technology for the black-on-black pottery.
403. ———. *The Ten Grandmothers*. Norman: University of Oklahoma
     Press, 1948.
     An odd book which contains fictionalized accounts from individuals
     about the "ten grandmothers," the sacred medicine bundles of the
     Kiowa—stories from men and women about the central symbology
     of the tribe.
404. "Mary Crawler." *Indians At Work*. 1 (December, 1935): 47.
     A short portrait of Mary Crawler, also called Moving Robe, re-
     puted to be the only woman who fought at the Little Big Horn.
405. Mason, Carol I. "Eighteenth Century Culture Change Among the
     Lower Creeks." *Florida Anthropology*. 16 (1963): 65-80.
     An examination of archaeological evidence which indicates that
     male Creeks were more profoundly affected by the fur trade than
     women—women were the continuing force for cultural conser-
     vation.
406. Mason, Otis. *Woman's Share In Primitive Cultures*. London and
     New York: MacMillan and Company, 1895.
     One of the earliest works which stressed women's positive and
     major roles in social, religious and economic life of tribal peoples—
     much about Native North America—very dated and naive in many
     ways.

407. Mason, Willa Faye. "An Investigation of the Relationship Between the Self-Concept and Physical Fitness of White, American Indian and Black Women College Students." Dissertation, University of Arkansas, 1979.

A physical education dissertation which compares attitudes of self to physical health, physical fitness and sports participation.

408. Matchett, William F. "Repeated Hallucinatory Experiences As A Part of the Mourning Process Among Hopi Women." *Psychiatry.* 35 (May, 1972): 185-94.

A very interesting description of a phenomenon that remains exotic only to Western-trained observers—not very substantive contribution.

409. Mathes, Valerie Shirer. "American Indian Women and the Catholic Church." *North Dakota History.* 47 (Fall, 1980): 20-25.

Details something of the lives of Indian female religious figures and the roles that Indian women have assumed in Catholic church activities on reservations.

410. ———. "A New Look at the Role Of Women in Indian Societies." *American Indian Quarterly.* 2, no.2 (1975): 131-39.

A work examining the traditional forms of autonomy and power among Native women—suggests reexamination of older scholarship.

411. ———. "Susan LaFlesche: Portrait for a Western Album." *American West.* 16, no.5-6 (1979): 38.

A very brief article about the physician and reformist lecturer, Suzanne LaFlesche—accompanied by the very fine photo that resides in the Nebraska Historical Archives.

412. Mathur, Mary E.F. (Iroquois). "Who Cares That A Woman's Work Is Never Done?" *Indian Historian.* 4, no.2 (1971): 11-16.

A comment on the traditional, historical work roles—their importance and a plea for further attention.

413. Matthews, Washington. "Navajo Weavers." *Bureau Of American Ethnology, 1881-82.* 3 (1884).

One of the first studies of Navajo weaving, complete with biographical and artistic profiles of several weavers.

414. Matthiasson, John S. "Northern Baffin Island Women in Three Cultural Periods." *Western Canadian Journal Of Anthropology.* 6, no.3 (1976): 201-12.
A fine article which attempts to correct the inherent sex bias in the previous literature on Inuit women by showing the women through three periods of historical and cultural change.

415. McCane-O'Connor, Mallory. "The Squaw As Artist: A Reevaluation." *Southern Quarterly.* 17, no. 2 (1979): 8-15.
An examination, however brief, of the role of Native women as artists, from prehistory to the present.

416. McCarty, Darlene (Spokane). "A Day With Yaha." In J.R. Milton, ed. *The American Indian Speaks.* Vermillion: University of South Dakota Press, 1969: 119-25.
A personal appreciation of a grandmother by a young woman.

417. McClary, Ben Harris. "Nancy Ward." *Tennessee Historical Quarterly.* (December, 1962).
A more serious and scholarly treatment than usually accorded Ward—still missing as full an accounting possible however.

418. McClung, Jacquetta. "The 80's, Decade for Indian Women." *Oklahomans for Indian Opportunity Journal.* (1980).
A brief article which outlines some of the enormous changes in Indian country and the consequent opportunities for Native women.

419. McCormack, Patricia, ed. *Western Canadian Journal Of Anthropology:* Special Issue on Cross-Sex Relations and Native Peoples. 6, no. 3 (1976).
A fine, essential volume with the bulk of articles on Native North American peoples—the best of revisionist scholarship on male-female, female-female relationships.

420. McDonald, Thomas. "Group Psychotherapy With Native American Women." *International Journal of Group Psychotherapy.* 25, no.4 (1975): 410-20.
A methodological description with comments especially interesting on group interaction between Native women in a therapeutic effort.

421. McElroy, Ann P. "Canadian Arctic Modernization and Change in Female Inuit Role Identification." *American Ethnologist.* 2 (1975): 662-86.

One of a series of articles by McElroy on the interaction between sex-role identity and adaptation in the arctic.

422. ———. "The Negotiation of Sex-Role Identity in Eastern Arctic Culture Change." *Western Canadian Journal Of Anthropology.* 6, no. 3 (1976): 184-200. A transactional model which explores the "patterns of male and female adaptation to culture change in the Eastern Canadian arctic."
Suggests that flexibility in sex-role identity determined adaptive success.

423. McRaye, Walter. *Pauline Johnson And Her Friends.* Toronto: The Ryerson Press, 1974.
One of several biographical treatments of the Mohawk poet and actress, Pauline Johnson—this one also includes her literary circle.

424. McSwain, Romola Mae. "The Role of Wives in the Urban Adjustment of Navajo Migrant Families to Denver, Colorado." *Navajo Urban Relocation Research Report.* 10 (April, 1965).
The thesis of this article is that women, particularly wives, play the key role in the families' urban readjustment.

425. Meachem, Alfred B. *Wi-ne-ma (The Woman Chief) and Her People.* Hartford, Connecticut: American Publishing Co., 1876; rep.1977.
An utterly biased interpretation of a non-Indian "heroine," overlaid with Christian rhetoric and a misunderstanding of true Native leadership.

426. Mead, Margaret. *The Changing Culture Of An Indian Tribe.* New York: Columbia University Press, 1932.
One of the first and most major studies of family life in a tribe—with major attentions paid to the roles and statuses of women, not simply in their roles as wives and mothers but as agents of change and stability.

427. Medicine, Beatrice (Sioux). "The Changing Dakota Family and the Stresses Therein." *Pine Ridge Research Bulletin.* 9 (1969): 1-20.
Some interesting reflections on change and on cultural and social stresses affecting women, men, children and families in a post-World War II reservation environment.

428. ———. "Ella C. Deloria: The Emic Voice." *Melus.* 7, no.4 (Winter, 1980): 23-30.

A short and interesting piece on the special contributions of Ella Deloria to Sioux scholarship.

429. ———. "The Interaction of Culture and Sex Roles In the Schools." In Dpt. of Ed./Nat'l. Inst. of Ed. *Conference On The Educational And Occupational Needs Of American Indian Women, 1976.* Washington, DC: GPO, 1980: 141-158.

A thoughful piece on the double bind of being Indian and female in schools.

430. ———. "Kunshilei (Grandmothers)." *Plainswoman.* (c. 1970).

A short article on the importance and role of grandmothers in Lakota Sioux and general Indian cultures.

431. ———. *The Native American Woman: A Perspective.* Albuquerque: ERIC/CRESS, 1978.

A general, derivative work on Native women, with a critique of historical and anthropological treatments and a plea for alternative approaches.

432. ———. "The Role of Women in Native American Societies: A Bibliography." *Indian Historian.* 8, no. 3 (1975): 51-53.

An early bibliographic effort confined mostly to ethnographic literature—Some errors, but offers an introduction to women in that ethnographic literature.

433. Metcalf, Ann. "The Effects of Boarding School on Navajo Self-Image and Maternal Behavior." Dissertation, Stanford University, 1975.

A culture-change thesis, showing the negative and positive impacts of a boarding school education on Navajo women—the precursor to a fine series of articles.

434. ———. "From Schoolgirl to Mother: The Effects of Education on Navajo Women." *Social Problems.* 23 (June, 1976): 535-44.

A sympathetic and insightful work on the effects of Western education on personal and cultural behavior among the Navajo.

435. ———. "Reservation-Born, City-Bred: Native American Women and Children in the City." In Ann McElroy and Carolyn Matthiasson, eds. *Sex-Roles In Changing Cultures.* Buffalo: State University of New York Press, 1980.

A focus on change and strategies for positive change and adaptation.

436. Metoyer-Duran, Cheryl (Cherokee). "The Native American Woman." In Elouise Snyder, ed. *The Study Of Women: Enlarging Perspectives On Social Reality.* New York: Harper and Row, 1979: A general look at modern conditions and traditional stereotypes.

437. Michelson, Truman, ed. "The Autobiography of a Fox Indian Woman." *U.S. Bureau of American Ethnology Papers.* 40 (1925): 295-349.
    The first in a series of three female autobiographies of Michelson, said to be somewhat spurious by tribespeople—interesting nevertheless from a much-studied tribe.

438. ———. "Narrative of A Southern Cheyenne Woman." Smithsonian Institution *Miscellaneous Collections.* 87 (1932): 51.
    One of several narratives collected and edited by Michelson—somewhat untrustworthy in terms of accurate reporting, but interesting nevertheless for comparison to other Cheyenne tales.

439. ———. "Narrative of an Arapaho Woman." *American Anthropologist.* 35 (1935): 595-610.
    One of three autobiographical narratives edited by Michelson, said to be inaccurately recorded, but interesting for its accounting from a little studied tribal group.

440. Miller, Dorothy I. (Blackfeet). "The Native American Family: The Urban Way." *Families Today.* 1 (1980): 441-83.
    A discussion of the urban Indian family, structures and changes, with special attention to the roles of women in cultural and structural maintenance.

441. ———. "Native American Women: Leadership Images." *Integrated Education.* 15 (January-February, 1978): 37-39.
    A brief analysis of leadership models and roles followed by Native women.

442. Miller, W.H., N. Sandoval (Pueblo) and E. Musholt. "Vocational and Personal Effectiveness Training of a Developmentally Delayed Navajo Girl." *White Cloud Journal.* 1, no. 1 (1978): 11-14.
    The account of therapy for a Navajo woman with vocational and personal problems.

443. Minor, Nono. "The American Indian: Famous Indian Women in Early America." *Real West Magazine.* (March, 1971): 35-78.

A completely popularized, shallow account of the same old historical figures—unreliable.

444. Misch, Jo. "Lilah D. Lindsay." *Chronicles Of Oklahoma.* 33 (1955): 193-201.

A biographical piece about the first Creek woman in the Territory to receive a college degree—she taught at Wealaka Mission School.

445. Monthan, Guy and Doris. "Dexter Quotskuyva Nampeyo." *American Indian Art Magazine.* (Autumn, 1977): 58-63.

A summary article on the life and work of this well-known Hopi polychrome pottery and potter.

446. ———. "Helen Cordero." *American Indian Art Magazine.* (Autumn, 1977): 72-76.

A sound retrospective article on the famed "storyteller" figure potter from Cochiti—a good introduction to the tension between tradition and modern art.

447. Mooney, Lucinda. "The American Indian Woman in Urban Education." *Urban Anthropology.* (Summer, 1977).

An anthropologically-based article which looks at the interlock between culture and change in an urban educational setting—good on women's roles in education.

448. Moore, Patricia A. "Indian Woman's Sterilization Suit Starts." *National Catholic Reporter.* (January 19, 1979): 16, Sec. 4.

A brief report on the initiation of suit by a Montana woman for wrongful sterilization.

449. Morrow, Terry. "LaDonna Harris: A Woman Who Gives A Damn." *Redbook.* 34 (1970): 75, 115, 117-18.

An early article about the Comanche politician and leader, LaDonna Harris, who founded Americans for Indian Opportunity, a major activist organization of the decade.

450. Mossiker, Frances. *Pocahontas: The Life And The Legend.* New York : Alfred E. Knopf, 1976.

One of the best biographies of Pocahontas—dealing with the myth, the legend, the known facts—good bibliography.

451. "Mother of Many Children." 16mm, Color/Sound, 80 minutes, 1980. Produced and directed by Alanis Obomsawin for the Nat'l. Film Bd. of Canada.

A fine, though ill-edited film, on Canadian Native women—their art, their music, the political rules that affect them.

452. Mulleneaux, May. "Factors in Navajo Culture That May Affect Their Acceptance of Prenatal Care." Thesis, University of Southern California, 1954.

A fairly rudimentary study of cultural attitudes that affect women's acceptance of Western prenatal care.

453. Murray, Janette K. "Ella Deloria: A Biographical Sketch and Literary Analysis." Dissertation, University of North Dakota, 1975.

A good summary and survey of the work of this major intellectual leader and scholar.

454. Nabokov, Peter, ed. *Native American Testimony: An Anthology Of Indian And White Relations: First Encounter to Dispossession.* New York: T.Y. Crowell and Co., 1978.

Several first-hand testimonies from Native women, a precursor to a complete volume yet unpublished.

455. Nahayama, Elijii. "Some Notes on a Woman of Aleut." *Anthropological Society Of Tokyo Journal.* 49 (1934): 23-29.

An anthropological/biographical approach—useful primarily because so little has been written on Aleut women.

456. Natatok, Nowya (Inuit). "Nowya Completes Her RNA Course." *Inuttitut.* (Autumn, 1972): 14-15.

An Inuit woman describes her entry into a nursing career.

457. "Navajo Girl." 16 mm, Color/Sound, 17 minutes, 1973. Produced by Bobwin Associates.

A children's film which shows something of traditional Navajo sheep-raising—also of weaving.

458. "The Navajos and Annie Wauneka." Produced by CBS News for the Twentieth Century Program.

A documentary of the Medal of Freedom-winning Annie Wauneka, and the life of public service she has devoted to the improvement of Navajo health.

459. "Navajos Film Themselves: A Series." Super 8, B and W, 22 minutes, 1968. Produced by John Adair and Sol Worth for the Center for Mass Communication.

In two films, the Benally's, a mother and daughter film each other in various tasks of weaving—a fascinating and unexpected view.

460. Neil, Wilfred T. "Bird Woman's Real Story." *The West.* 9 (July/August, 1968).
     Less "reality" than the title suggests about Sacajawea.
461. Nelson, Ann Thrift. "Native Women's Ritual Sodalities in Native North America." *Western Canadian Journal Of Anthropology.* 6, no. 3 (1976): 29-67.
     A unique and very good introductory work, though theoretically dense, which connects the presence and power of female sodalities (formal female groupings with ritual roles) with economic behavior.
462. Nelson, Mary Carroll. *Annie Wauneka.* Minneapolis: Dillon Press, 1972.
     One in a series of good biographies about modern and historical Native leaders.
463. ———. *Daisy Hooe Nampeyo, Pueblo.* Minneapolis, MN: Dillon Press, 1978.
     A children's biography—part of a series—on the contemporary Pueblo artist and potter Daisy Nampeyo.
464. ———. *Maria Martinez.* Minneapolis: Dillon Press, 1972.
     About the famous artist and potter—one of a series for children about Native leaders and cultural figures.
465. ———. *Pablita Velarde.* Minneapolis: Dillon Press, 1971.
     About the well-known Santa Clara Pueblo artist—one in a good series for children.
466. "The Netsilek Eskimo: Film Series." 16mm, Color/Sound, 8 parts, 1963-65. Produced by the National Film Board of Canada.
     This extensive filming shows a Netsilek Inuit family as they work, relate, struggle—more about women and women's roles in this general film than in any other intensive effort.
467. New Mexico People and Energy Collective (Tom Barry, Deb Preutsch, Beth Wood). *Red Ribbons For Emma.* Stanford, CA: New Seed Press, 1981.
     A children's book about Emma Yazzie's fight against coal development in Navajo country—fictional but valid.
468. Newberger, Richard. "Was Sacajawea Really the Guide of Lewis and Clark?" *Inland Empire Magazine, Spokesman Review.* (July 6, 1952).

Another of the seemingly endless debates—without resolution—
over whether the Bird Woman was really a guide to Lewis and
Clark.

469. Niethammer, Carolyn. *Daughters Of The Earth: The Lives And
Legends Of Native American Women.* New York: MacMillan and
Co., 1977.
A nicely illustrated, informative but uncritical collage of information from often obscure anthropological sources—on rite, behavior, role—a decent introduction and ethnographic bibliography.

470. North American Indian Women's Association. "Special Needs of
Handicapped Indian Children and Indian Women's Problems."
Washington, DC: Bureau of Indian Affairs, 1978.
A report from NAIWA about the needs of handicapped children,
pregnant women and communities where there is child abuse—a
rudimentary but interesting report.

471. "North American Indians Today Series: Maria of the Pueblos."
16mm, Color/Sound, 4 films, c. 1970. No production data available. A history of San Ildefonso pottery making along with Maria's
contributions to art and to her people.

472. O'Meara, Walter. *Daughters Of The Country: The Women Of The
Fur Trades And Mountain Men.* New York: Harcourt, Brace and
World, 1968.
A focus on the "rugged" men of the Trans-Mississippi West and
the stereotyped women, many Native, who shared their lives—a
shallow book.

473. O'Neale, Lula M. "Yurok-Karok Basket Weavers." *University Of
California Publications In American Archaeology And Ethnology.*
32 (1932): 1-84.
A fairly detailed early presentation of Northern California basket-
making and basketmakers.

474. Oakland, Lynn and Robert Kane. "The Working Mother and Child
Neglect On the Navajo Reservation." *Pediatrics.* 51 (May, 1973):
849-53.
A work which clearly outlines changing Navajo family patterns
and sex-role changes as well, though its intent is to demonstrate
something about the neglect of children by working mothers.

475. *Ohoyo: A Bulletin For American Indian/Alaska Native Women.* Wichita Falls, Texas: Ohoyo Resource Center, 1979-1982.

Edited by Owanah Anderson (Choctaw), this regular periodic publication prints news about native women in the US and Canada—from a federally-funded native women's project that seeks to secure educational and economic equity for Native women—other publications.

476. Opland, David V. "Marriage and Divorce for the Devil's Lake Reservation." *North Dakota Law Review.* 47, no. 2 (1971): 317-34.

A fairly straightforward descriptive survey of divorce patterns on this North Dakota Sioux reservation—from a legal perspective in state court terms.

477. Opler, Morris E. "Cause and Effect in Apachean Agriculture, Division of Labor, Residence Patterns and Girl's Puberty Rites." *American Anthropologist.* 74 (1972): 1133-46.

A speculative article that makes connections between economic behavior, patterns of residence, ceremonial behavior—controversial (Driver, 1972).

478. Orvis, Brian. "Amy (Clemens/Pequis) Greets The Queen." *Tawow* 1 (Autumn, 1970): 30-31.

Social page news from Canada interesting for its portrayal of white-Indian interactions and expectations.

479. Oswalt, Robert L., ed. *Kashaya Texts.* University of California Publications in Linguistics. 36 (1964).

Much in this volume from Pomo women and a great deal from Essie Parrish, the noted "dreamer" and healer.

480. Oswalt, Wendell H. "Traditional Storyknife Tales of the Yuk Girls." *Proceedings Of The American Philosophical Society.* 108 (1964): 310-36.

A presentation of a number of traditional Yuk tales, told by young women.

481. Owen, F. Carrington. "Improving Nursing Skills—A Program for Indian Women." *Nursing Outlook.* 19, no. 4 (1971): 258-59.

A brief description of a program directed primarily toward the training of Indian LPN's and non-degree nurses.

482. Owen, Robert Dale. "Pocahontas, or An Historical Drama." New York: George Dearborn, 1837.

Yet another of the many plays about Pocahontas—this time by an American utopian philosopher who offers some interesting political interpretive twists on the same old Pocahontas story.

483. Owens, Narcissa (Cherokee). *Memoirs Of Narcissa Owens*. Seattle: University of Washington Press, 1907.

The curious remembrances of an upper-class, Christian, well-educated Cherokee woman.

484. Pandey, Trilokey Nath. "Flora Zuni, Zuni, 1897-." In Margot Liberty, ed. *American Indian Intellectuals*. St. Paul, Minnesota: West Publishing Co., 1978.

A very fine article on a figure important both to her tribe and to non-Indian scholars—Zuni as teacher, consultant, cultural revitalist.

485. Parker, Seymour. "Eskimo Psychopathology In the Context of Eskimo Personality and Culture." *American Anthropologist*. 64 (1962): 72-96.

A standard personality-and-culture work dealing in a major way with female manifestations of "psychopathological" behavior.

486. Parkman, E. Breck. "The Maien." *National Women's Anthropology Newsletter*. 5, no. 2 (1981): 16-22.

A brief presentation on Coastal Miwok female leaders—religious, spiritual, political—helpful work on a tribe so little studied.

487. Parrish, Otis (Pomo) and Paula Hammett. "Parrish: A Pomo Shaman." *Native Self-Sufficiency*. 6 (1981): 8-9.

An appreciation of the noted dreamer and healer by her son—connects nicely with filmed materials on Parrish (1962, 1964).

488. Parsons, Elsie Clews. "Mothers and Children at Zuni, New Mexico." *Man*. 19 (November, 1919): 168-73.

One in a series of early articles by Parsons describing mother-child relationships and child-rearing patterns—minimally informative for contemporary readers.

489. ———. "Tewa Mothers and Children." *Man*. 24 (October, 1924): 148-51.

Another in a series of descriptive articles on maternal behavior, child rearing and mother-child relationships—a frail reference.

490. ———. "Waiyautitsa of Zuni, New Mexico." *Scientific Monthly.* 9 (1919): 443-57.

A fascinating description of a powerful and important female figure at Zuni—one of the early anthropological biographies.

491. Paul, Frances Lackey (Tlingit). *Katahah.* Anchorage: Alaska Northwest Publishing Co.,1976.

A romanticized and fictionalized reconstruction of a 19th century Tlingit girl's life, based on Paul's life—interesting and entertaining.

492. ———. *My Most Unforgettable Character: A Memoir Of Matilda Kinsion Paul-Tamaree, Tlingit.* Juneau, Alaska: privately published, 1978.

A short memorial piece for a mother—useful because of the importance of the family in Southern Alaska.

493. Peabody, Elizabeth. *Sarah Winnemucca's Practical Solution To The Indian Problem.* Boston: privately printed, 1886.

A 19th century social reform tract—a biased, but interesting defense of Winnemucca's brand of activism and political sense.

494. ———. *The Second Report Of The Model School Of Winnemucca.*

One of several admiring reformist reports for the educational reform work of the Paiute nationalist—work that has some currency in modern Indian education.

495. Peet, Stephen D. "The Indian Woman As She Was." *American Antiquarian And Oriental Journal.* 27 (1905): 348-50.

The American Indian woman as outside viewers wished her to be, with the domestic sphere set aside for women, the "forest" for the men—antiquarian well describes this author's early interests.

496. Pence, Mary Lou. "Ellen Hereford Washakie of the Shoshones." *Annals Of Wyoming.* 22 (July, 1950): 3-11.

A rare piece on a Shoshone woman of some significance in her community.

497. Perkinson, Mary O. "The Development of Weaving As A Possible Satisfying Home Industry Among the Pueblos." Thesis, University of Kentucky, 1945.

One of the post-war efforts at economic development of indigenous craft—so successful in the mountain South—now tried in Indian country.

498. Perry, Richard J. "The Fur Trade and the Status of Women in the Western Subarctic." *Ethnohistory*. 26, no. 4 (1979): 363-76.
A speculative and interesting article on the relationship of fur trade domestic relations and activities to the status of women.

499. ———. "Variations on the Female Referent in Athabaskan Cultures." *Journal Of Anthropological Research*. 33 (1977): 99-119.
One of the more stimulating linguistic analyses, based on cultural data, on the significance of "femaleness" and the female domains of power and status.

500. Peterson, Jacqueline L. "The People In Between: Indian-White Marriage and the Generation of a Metis Society and Culture in the Great Lakes Region, 1680-1830." Dissertation, University of Illinois/Chicago Circle, 1981.
An extraordinarily provocative and useful work on the Indian women who married trappers and traders, the children they raised and the Mixed-blood society that changed the shape of history and culture in the Great Lakes.

501. Peterson, Susan. *The Living Tradition of Maria Martinez*. Tokyo: Kodansha International, 1977.
The latest and most definitive artistic study of Maria and her family—their contributions to revitalistic tradition in Pueblo pottery and to pottery internationally—a good bibliography.

502. Philip, Kenneth. *John Collier's Crusade For Indian Reform, 1920-1954*. Tucson: University of Arizona Press, 1977.
One of the first critical examinations of the Indian New Deal—with a long look at Alice Lee Jemison's brand of Iroquois nationalism. The opening shot in revisionist history of John Collier's administration.

503. ———. "Raw Deal, the Iroquois of New York View The Indian Reorganization Act." *Anthropology*. 2 (September, 1978).
More on Alice Lee Jemison and the Seneca stand against John Collier's policies.

504. "Pictures Out of My Life." 16mm, Color/Sound, c.1965. Produced by Wolf Koenig for the National Film Board Of Canada.
A filmed version of Pitseolak's pictorial autobiography, with animated versions of her autobiographical portraits and a voice-over by the artist.

505. Pine, Charles J. (Choctaw). "Suicide in American Indian and Alaskan Native Tradition." *White Cloud Journal.* 2, no.3 (1981): 3-8.

An extremely interesting article examining the roots of suicide in traditional behavior and offering extensive data on differing male and female traditions in different tribal groupings.

506. Pitseolak (Inuit). *Pictures Out Of My Life.* New York: Design Collaborative Books and Oxford University Press, 1971.

The pictorial and narrative autobiography of a beloved and well-known Inuit artist who had a cult following among non-Native collectors—unornamented and beautiful artistically.

507. "Plains Indian Girl." 16mm, Color/Sound, 13 minutes, c. 1965. Produced by Carlin Films.

Shows the life of a contemporary girl living in the Missouri River Basin on a reservation—generally low quality.

508. Pokagon, Simon (Algonquin). *Queen Of The Woods.* Berrien Springs, Michigan: Hardscrabble Press, 1979; rep. from 1899.

One of the earliest novels by Native writers—essentially a romantic, European love story between a Native man and woman—interesting in choice of theme and treatment by an Indian author.

509. Polingaysi, Elizabeth Qoyawayma (Hopi) with Vada Carlson. *No Turning Back.* Albuquerque: University of New Mexico Press, 1977.

The narrative of Elizabeth White, a distinguished potter who revitalized some traditional styles and technologies—shows the extraordinary influence of Christianity on many lives.

510. "Pomo Shaman." 16mm, B and W, 20 minutes, 1963. Produced by the Univ. of Cal. Media Extension Ctr.

Shows a healing ceremony conducted by Essie Parrish, the noted Pomo healer and dreamer—film quality awful, but the ceremony is unique on film in that it does show a female healer at work.

511. Powers, Marla N. "Menstruation and Reproduction: An Oglala Case." *Signs, A Journal Of Women And Culture.* 6, no.1 (Fall, 1980): 54-63.

A fine work which treats menstruation, puberty rites and reproduction as Native people understand them—noting the positive functions these rites and functions play in Native women's lives.

512. Price, Anna/Her Eyes Grey (Apache). "Personal Narrative of Anna Price." In Keith Basso, ed. *Western Apache Raiding And Warfare.* Tucson: University of Arizona Press, 1971.
     One of several available narratives, from a woman's perspective, on tribal warfare.

513. Primack, W. "Family Planning at Pine Ridge." *Pine Ridge Research Bulletin.* (1968): 11-17.
     A description of the problems and outcomes of a reservation-based family planning service.

514. Randle, Martha C. "Iroquois Women, Then and Now." In William N. Fenton, ed. *Bureau Of American Ethnology Bulletin. 149, Anthropology Papers: Symposium On Local Diversity In Iroquois Culture.* 8 (1951): 167-80.
     One of the earliest revisionist articles on the status of Iroquois women.

515. Rapp, Rayna. "Review Essay: Anthropology." *Signs: A Journal Of Women And Culture In Society.* 4, no. 3 (1979): 497-513.
     A review essay of recent literature on the anthropology of women— very helpful for evaluating anthropological work on Indian women.

516. Reed, T.B. "Cries-For-Salmon, A Tena Woman." In Elsie Clews Parsons, ed. *American Indian Life.* Lincoln: University of Nebraska Press, 1920: 337-62.
     A biographical work intended to "reveal the culture" of a then modern woman.

517. Rees, John E. "Madame Charbonneau, The Indian Woman Who Accompanied the Lewis and Clark Expedition: How She Received Her Indian Name and What Became of Her." Salmon, Idaho: The Lemhi City Historical Society Ms., 1970.
     A strange memorial treatment, more folklore than history.

518. Reichard, Gladys. *Desba, Woman Of The Desert.* New York: JJ Augustin, 1939; rep. 1971.
     An extensive artistic and ethnological autobiography of a Navajo weaver—meant to reveal the rural Navajo culture as well as the life of this woman.

519. ———. *Spider Woman: A Story Of Navajo Weavers And Chanters.* New York: MacMillan and Co., 1934; rep. 1968.

One in a series of Reichard's works on Navajo women artists, this one including some study of "singers" or healers, male and female, who chant the songs given by Spider Woman, the first "Mother."

520. Reid, Russell. "Sakakawea." *North Dakota History.* 30 (April-July, 1963): 101-13.

One of the many articles on the Shoshone woman—repeats the same tired information.

521. Richards, Cara E. "Matriarchy or Mistake: The Role of Iroquois Women Through Time." In Verne F. Ray, ed. *Cultural Stability And Cultural Change.* Seattle: American Ethnological Society, 1957: 30-45.

The best of the revisionist articles on the Iroquois matriarchy, showing the vast historical and cultural changes affecting women.

522. ———. "The Role of Iroquois Women: A Study of the Onandaga Reservation." Dissertation, Cornell University, 1957.

A specific reservation study of Iroquois women,balancing out the myth and the realities of modern life and demonstrating the specific changes in role and ritual life throughout a period of time.

523. Rickert, Herbert, Owen Chuculate and Dorothy Klinert. "Aging and Ethnicity in Healthy Elderly Women." *Geriatrics.* 26, no. 5 (1971): 146-52.

An article which makes extensive comments on Indian women— some interesting comments on Indian views of health, aging and elderly women.

524. Rickey, Eleanor. "Sagebrush Princess With A Cause." *American West.* 12 (November, 1975): 30-33, 57-63.

A contemporary update on Sarah Winnemucca Hopkins and her activities on behalf of Paiute survival.

525. Riddell, William Renwick. "The Sad Tale of An American Indian Wife." *Journal Of The American Academy Of Criminal Law And Criminology.* 13, no.1 (1922): 82-89.

A rather sentimental, but grim legal report on an abused woman— the story of her attempt to get redress through the law.

526. Riggs, Mary Ann Clare and Eliza Marpi-cokawin (Sioux). *Raratonwan Oyato en Wipiye sa: qa Sara Warpanica qon: A Narrative Of Pious Indian Women.* Boston: Crocker and Brewster, 1842.

The title is more than sufficient to describe this work about Christian Native women—a short tract really.

527. Robertson, Wyndham. *Pocahontas, Alias Matoaka And Her Descendents.* Baltimore, Maryland: Geneological Publishing Company, 1968; rep. from 1887.
A geneological tree, for all those Virginians and others who claim descendency from the American Indian "princess"—made for those who wish to establish an American royal line.

528. Robin, Enid Fenton. "Indian Girl, White Girl." Thesis, Columbia University, 1943.
A comparison between Pomo and white girls in California, not especially informative.

529. Robinson, William G. "Sahakawea-Sacajawea-When and Where Did the Indian Bird Woman Die and Where Was She Buried?" *The Wiiyohi* (South Dakota Historical Society). 10 (September, 1956).
One more piece about the long-standing dispute over Sacajawea's death place and age at death.

530. Roessel, Ruth (Navajo). *Women In Navajo Society.* Rough Rock, Arizona: Navajo Resource Center, 1981.
A good, basic and interesting account of the mythological and societal roles of Navajo women—their present status and problems.

531. Rothenberg, Diane. "Erosion of Power: An Economic Basis for the Selective Conservatism of Seneca Women in the Nineteenth Century." *Western Canadian Journal Of Anthropology.* 6, no.3 (1976): 106-22.
Says women's conservatism was strategy to control subsistence distribution.

532. Royal Canadian Government. *Indian Women And The Law In Canada: Citizens Minus.* Ottawa: Canadian Government Publishing Centre, 1978.
An historical and psychological study of the Canadian law and its impacts on Native women who marry non-status and non-Indian men—the factors which continue to influence both Indian leaders and government to leave the Indian Act unrevised.

533. Royal Commission on the Status of Women. *Study And Field Research On Native Women.* Edmonton, Alberta: Royal Commission on the Status of Women, 1968.

One of several helpful status reports from Canada, useful for comparison to conditions.

534. *Sacajawea, Guide Of The Lewis And Clark Expedition.* Glendale, Ca.: Arthur H. Clark Co., 1933; rep. 1957.

The first "authoritative," but terribly frail history of the Bird Woman—interesting but not very reliable.

535. Salerno, Nan and Rosamond Vanderburgh. *Shaman's Daughter.* Englewood Cliffs, New Jersey: Prentice-Hall, Inc., 1980.

One of the best modern novels about Native women—about a turn-of-the century Ojibwa herbalist, basketmaker and community leader. Moving and compelling in a low-keyed way.

536. Sanders, Douglas. "Indian Women: A Brief History of Their Roles and Rights." *McGill Law Journal.* 21, no.4 (1975): 656-72.

A good description of the varying historical forms of treatment of Native women, especially mixed-blood women, in Canada—includes a fine account of the body of Canadian law applicable to them.

537. Sapiel, Madas (Penobscot-Passamaquoddy). "We Don't Make Baskets Anymore: Memories of Madas Sapiel." *Salt: A Journal Of Northeast Culture.* 4, no.4 (1979): 4-16.

A narrative from a traditional woman who has seen much change in her tribe—some considerable discussion of traditional basket-making practices and their relative disappearance.

538. Sapir, Edward, ed. *Takelma Texts.* University of Pennsylvania Anthropological Publications From the University *Museum.* 2, no. 1 (1901): 1-267.

Most of these early texts taken from Frances Johnson, a female narrator.

539. ———. *Yana Texts.* New York: Kraus Reprint Co., 1964.

Extensive collection of traditional Yana tales from Betty Brown, narrator.

540. Sauceda, Judith Brostoff. "From the Inner Circle: The Relationship of the Space Occupied, Past and Present By Southwestern Amer-

ican Indian Women to the Indo-Hispanic women of Yesteryear
and Today." Dissertation, University of Colorado at Boulder, 1979.
A study of ethnic and gender-based use of inner and outer space.

541. Schaefer, Ann Eastlake. "The Status of Iroquois Women." Thesis,
University of Pennsylvania, 1925.
Another early and unenlightening thesis on Iroquois women.

542. Schaefer, Dana and Mark Friedman. "To Sing the Song of the
Mother: An Interview With Ok Shenneh." *Art In Humanity*. 3
(February, 1977): 2-5.
More drama than art in this over-romanticized interview with an
artist.

543. Schaeffer, Claude E. "The Kutenai Female Berdache: Courier, Guide,
Prophetess and Warrior." *Ethnohistory*. 12 (Summer, 1965): 193-
236.
One of the very few works on a specific female berdache tradition,
this one with regard to the role and deeds of a particular figure.

544. Scheirbeck, Helen Maynor (Lumbee). "Current Educational Status
of American Indian Girls." In Dpt. of Ed./Nat'l. Inst. of Ed.
*Conference On The Educational And Occupational Needs Of
American Indian Women, 1976.* Washington, DC: GPO, 1980:63-
82.
A solid assessment of the educational status and needs of younger
women.

545. Schlegel, Alice. "The Adolescent Socialization of the Hopi Girl."
Ethnology. 12, no. 4 (1973): 449-62.
A good article showing the process through which a female learns
the roles and responsibilities of an adult Hopi woman—includes
good information on complementarity in roles.

546. ———. "Male and Female in Hopi Thought and Action." In Alice
Schlegel, ed. *Sexual Stratification: A Cross-Cultural View.* New
York: Columbia University Press, 1978.
A very useful and provocative article detailing the notions of male
and female in Hopi understanding—poses a theory of mutual
dependency.

547. ———. "Sexual Antagonism Among the Sexually Egalitarian Hopi."
Ethos. 7, no. 2 (1979).

An interesting exploration of the ways in which sexual and role tensions are released in a society which stresses mutual dependencies.

548. Schneider, David M. and Kathleen Gough, eds. *Matrilineal Kinship.* Berkeley: University of California Press, 1961.

Much about the different forms of matriorganization and about Native North American tribal peoples in this standard reference on the topic.

549. Schultz, Amelia Louise. "Indian Unmarried Mothers." Thesis, University of Washington, 1947.

A thesis concerned with social work among Indian unmarried mothers—an unimpressive work.

550. Schultz, James Willard. *Bird Woman (Sacajawea): The Guide Of Lewis And Clark.* Boston: Houghton Mifflin, 1918.

One of the earliest book-length works that set the standards for the popular-folkloric history of the Shoshone woman.

551. ———. *My Life As An Indian: The Story Of A Red Woman And A White Man In The Lodges Of The Blackfeet.* Boston: Houghton Mifflin, 1907.

The subtitle says it all about this turn-of-the-century work by a furtrader and trapper who married a Blackfeet woman.

552. Scott, Lalla. *Karnee: Paiute Narrative.* Las Vegas: University of Nevada Press, 1966.

An "as-told-to" autobiography of only moderate interest since the author appears only to have asked for cultural and historical data and ignored a genuine personal account.

553. Scott, Leslee M. "Indian Women As Food Providers and Tribal Councilors." *Oregon History.* 42 (1941): 208-19.

An article which asserts that most tribal women derived their authority and power within the tribe from their essential and major role as food providers and dividers.

554. Scruton, David L. "Sex Differentiation in Memory Rentention of Aboriginal Behavior Patterns." Dissertation, University of Washington, 1954.

A study of memory retention and the differences between males and females on the Muckleshoot reservation.

555. Scully, Vincent. "In Praise of Women: The Mescalero Puberty." *Art In America.* 60 (July-August, 1972): 70-77.

A heavily photographic essay about the drama and art of the puberty ceremony—a kind of artistic travelogue.

556. "A Season of Grandmothers." Videotape, Color/Sound, 25 minutes, c. 1975. Produced by Circle Films.

Part of a series filmed by a Native company, this one focuses on winter and storytelling season, and on the grandmothers who tell the stories and raise children—a lovely film.

557. Seibert, Jerry. *Sacajawea, Guide To Lewis And Clark.* Boston: Houghton Mifflin and Co., 1960.

A very late and characteristically mundane work, repeating the known and honoring the unknown about Sacajawea.

558. Seymour, Flora. *Women of Trail And Wigwam.* New York: The Women's Press, 1930.

Popular biographical sketches of known and unknown Native women of the 18th and 19th centuries.

559. Sharp, Henry S. *Chipewyan Marriage.* Canadian Ethnological Service *Papers*/Nat'l Museum of Man. 58 (1979).

A long monograph on the structure, variants, and cultural forms of Chipewyan marriage.

560. Shaw, Anna Moore (Pima). *A Pima Past.* Tucson; University of Arizona Press, 1974.

Another "Christian" autobiography from the Southwest—interesting partly because of the rarely-studied Pima women and partly because the author has an eye for good detail.

561. Shipek, Florence. *The Autobiography Of Delphina Cuero.* Morongo Indian Reservation: Malki Museum Press, 1968; rep. 1970.

A classic—one of the best of the women's autobiography from a California Digueno. Delphina Cuero was a healer who documented her own life along with the tragic story of the Digueno.

562. Shirk, Lucyl A. "Muriel H. Wright: A Legend." *Chronicles Of Oklahoma.* (Fall, 1975): 397-99.

Another appreciation of Wright after her death in 1974—appropriate in the journal she founded.

563. Shore, James H. and Dennis Stone. "Duodenal Ulcer Among Northwest Coastal Indian Women." *American Journal Of Psychiatry.* 130 (July, 1973): 774-77.

A work on the effects of stress and change on the physical health of Northwest Coastal women—shows a high ulcer rate in these communities among women.

564. Shukry (Hamamsy), Laila Sayid. "The Role of Women in a Changing Navajo Society." Dissertation, Cornell University, 1954.

The dissertation on which Shukry's published work (Hamamsy, 1957) is based—longer and more detailed.

565. Sicherman, Barbara et al, eds. *Notable American Women.* Vol. IV. Cambridge: Harvard/Belknap, 1980.

Short biographical pieces on Muriel Wright by Ruth Arrington (Creek) and on Ella Deloria by Ray DeMallie—good especially for their contributions to scholarship.

566. Simpson, Richard. *OOTI: A Maidu Legacy.* Millbrae, California: Celestial Arts, 1979.

A beautifully ilustrated book with a frail and moving narrative from Lizzie Enos of the frail and tiny Maidu tribe—good for its description of her words and memories.

567. Sims, Hollis Jean. "A Study to Identify and Evaluate the Attitudes Toward Obesity Among Three Ethnic Groups of Women in Oklahoma: Black, White and Indian." Dissertation, University of Oklahoma, 1979.

A highly descriptive title of this study which seeks to examine concepts about obesity with respect to concepts about health care, beauty.

568. "Sioux Woman Awarded Achievement Medal." *Indians At Work.* (September-October, 1943): 26.

The news account of Ella Deloria's receipt of an award—interesting because of so few accounts of women in this BIA journal.

569. Sirdofsky, Arthur. "An Apache Girl Comes of Age." *Travel.* 138 (July, 1972): 40-43.

An illustrated travelogue on Apache girl's puberty ceremonies—author makes a tourist attraction out of the rite.

570. Skold, Betty W. *Sacajawea.* Minneapolis: Dillon Press, 1977.

A fairly straightforward treatment of the Bird Woman in a children's biography series noted for its uniform quality—manages to rise above the usually poor scholarship.

571. Slemenda, Charles W. "Sociocultural Factors Affecting Acceptance of Family Planning Services by Navajo Women." *Human Organization*. 37, no. 2 (1978): 190-94.

An attempt at analysis of those factors which determine receptivity of Native women toward Western health care and contraception.

572. Slocumb, John C., Charles Odoroff and Stephen Kunitz. "The Use-Effectiveness of Two Contraceptive Methods in a Navajo Population: The Problem of Program Dropouts." *American Journal Of Obstetrics And Gynecology*. 122, no. 6 (1975): 717-26.

A straightforward article on two contraceptive methods and which one works.

573. Smith, Dana Margaret/Mrs. White Mountain Smith (Hopi). *Hopi Girl*. Palo Alto, California: Stanford University Press, 1931.

An autobiographical novel about a girl between-two worlds—that of her traditional parents and white boarding schools.

574. Smith, John. *The History Of Travaille In Virginia Brittania*. London: The Hakluyt Society, 1624; rep. 1849.

The original story of his salvation by Pocahontas from Captain Smith, along with numerous other impressions about the Natives of Virginia.

575. Smithson, Carma Lee. *The Havasupai Woman*. New York: Johnson Reprint Corporation, 1959.

A valuable and under-valued study, useful for its detail and for its descriptions of Havasupai life drawn from the women themselves.

576. "Snakes Found Her Charming." *View, The Post-Crescent Magazine*. Appleton Wisc. (August 8, 1971): 1-4.

An intriguing tale of a Menomini woman who worked for years as a carnival snake charmer and entertainer.

577. Speare, Jean. *The Days Of Augusta*. North Pomfret, Vermont: David and Charles, 1975; rep. 1977.

A slim photographic essay with the reminiscences of an elderly woman of unidentified tribe—an often funny, sad memory framed in a funny and sometimes exhuberant description of present-day life.

578. Speck, Frank G. "The Case of Santu." *Papers Of The Museum Of The American Indian.* (1922): 55-70.

Micmac and Beothuck tales from Santu, a female narrator—interesting stories from a source believed by scholars to be somewhat spurious.

579. ———. *Catawba Texts.* New York: AMS Press, 1934; rep. 1964.

All female narrators in this volume.

580. Spindler, Louise S. "Menomini Women and Culture Change." *American Anthropological Association Memoirs.* No.1, Pt. 2. 64, no. 91 (1962): 1-113.

One in a series of works that documents the changing roles of women in times of great change and stress—suggests that women fare better than men.

581. ———. "Sixty-One Rorschachs and Fifteen Expressive Autobiographical Interviews of Menomini Women." In Bert Kaplan, ed. *Primary Records In Culture And Personality.* Madison, Wisconsin: Microcard Foundation, 1957.

Here, the interviews are much more interesting than testing or analysis.

582. Spindler, Louise S. and George D. "Male and Female Adaptation in Culture Change." *American Anthropologist.* 60 (April, 1958): 217-33.

Discusses the various modes of male and female adaptation to culture change—much information on Native North America—and suggests in general that females fare better than males under the stress of change.

583. Spindler, Mary Louise. "Women and Culture Change: A Study of the Menomini Indian." Dissertation, Stanford University, 1956.

A longer and more complete study on which Spindler's published work (1957, 1958, 1962) is based.

584. Stanley, Mrs. Andrew (Apache). "Personal Narrative of Mrs. Andrew Stanley." In Keith Basso, ed. *Western Apache Raiding And Warfare.* Tucson: University of Arizona Press, 1971.

Another warfare narrative from a woman's perspective—useful.

585. Starr, M.L. "She Did Not Lead a Movement." *American History Illustrated.* 15 (August, 1980): 44-47.

The illustrated story of a Crow woman chief and warrior—not very substantial, but interesting.

586. Steiner, Stan. "The Changing Woman." In *The New Indians.* New York: Harper and Row, 1960.

Chapter on Indian women in the political movements of the sixties— shows their major roles in fishing rights, land claims movements.

587. ————. *Spirit Woman: The Diaries Of Bonita Calachaw Nuñez, An American Indian.* San Francisco and New York: Harper and Row, 1979.

An interesting but diversionary presentation from an utterly eccentric woman, raised by wealthy whites—an artist sympathetic to Indian causes.

588. Stephens, William N. "A Cross-Cultural Study of Menstrual Taboos." *Genetic Psychology Monographs.* 64 (1961): 385-416.

A great deal on Native North American behaviors in this comparative article which misses much on positive attitudes toward menstruation.

589. Stewart, Irene (Navajo). *A Voice In Her Tribe: A Navajo Woman's Own Story.* Socorro, New Mexico: Ballena Press, 1980.

A very welcome, new autobiography from a Navajo woman with a politically and culturally active life in the tribe—a valuable book which details some of the realities of modern Navajo reservation life.

590. "Sucking Doctor." 16 mm, B and W, 45 minutes, 1964. Produced by W.R. Heick for the Univ. of Cal. Media Extension Center.

One in a series about the Pomo and about Essie Parrish, their healer and "dreamer." This focuses on Parrish and her healing practice.

591. Swader, Ruthe Anne Myers (Ojibwa). *The Anishinabe Woman.* Grand Marais, Minnesota: Independent School District 166, 1977.

A good work for teachers and students on Ojibwa women, their roles, their statuses, their contributions.

592. Szasz, Margaret Connell. " 'Poor Richard' Meets the Native American: Schooling for Young Indian Women in Eighteenth Century

Connecticut." *Pacific Historical Review.* XLIX, no.2 (1980): 215-35.

A very fine piece, from a general work on Indian education, about a group educated by the founder of Dartmouth College—a unique contribution.

593. Taber, Ronald W. "Sacajawea and the Suffragettes." *Pacific Northwest Quarterly.* (January, 1967).

An unusual and welcome contribution on the Sacajawea literature—detailing the suffragist request for a memorial statue and the resultant clamor over that request.

594. Tanner, Helen Hornbeck. "Coocoochee, Mohawk Medicine Woman." *American Indian Culture And Research Journal.* 3, no.3 (1979): 23-42.

An impeccable scholarly treatment of an historical figure of some interest—one of the few historical, contextual treatments of medicine women.

595. Taylor, Cora Alice. "The Social and Religious Status of Siouan Women Studied in the Light of the History and Environment of the Siouan Indian." Thesis, University of Kansas, 1906.

An attempt to counteract the stereotypes of the Plains woman as a burden-bearing drudge—ineffective and dull.

596. Temkin, Merle, Carol Stern and Margie Bowker. "Listening to Native American Women." *Heresies 13: Feminism and Ecology.* 4, no.1 (1981): 17-21.

A set of interviews with Rocky Olguin, Lois Red Elk and Madonna Thunderhawk on Indian women and their activist roles in energy- and environmentally-related protest and activism.

597. Temkin-Greener, Helene et al. "Surgical Fertility Regulation Among Women On The Navajo Indian Reservation." *American Journal Of Public Health.* 71, no. 4 (1981): 403-07.

A survey of surgical fertility regulation from 1972-78—describing the pattern of and reasons for surgery—male and female.

598. Terrell, John Upton and Donna Terrell. *Indian Women Of The Western Morning: Their Lives In Early America.* New York: Anchor Books, 1976.

A flimsy, unreliable narrative on Indian women and their work and roles in the past.

599. Theisz, R.D., ed. *Buckskin Tokens: Contemporary Oral Narratives Of The Lakota.* Aberdeen, South Dakota: Sinte Gleska College/ North Plains Press, 1975.

Folktales and personal narratives from Kate Blue Thunder, Irene Clairmont, and Christine Dunham among others.

600. Thorp, Rowena Weirauch. "The Dress of Plains Indian Women and Children." Thesis, Southern Methodist University, 1929.

The guide to basic buckskin and beadwork clothing on the Plains— a home economics thesis.

601. Thorpe, Dagmar (Sac and Fox). "Native Political Organizing in Nevada: A Woman's Perspective." *Native Self-Sufficiency.* 6 (1981): 14-15.

Some interview and analysis material on women's roles and perspectives in MX-Missile opposition.

602. Ticasuk, Emily Ivanoff Brown (Inuit). *The Roots Of Ticasuk: An Eskimo Woman's Family Story.* Anchorage: Alaska Northwest Publishing Company, 1981.

One of the few autobiographical studies from an Inuit family— interesting because of the importance of whole-family history.

603. Topper, Martin D. "Drinking Patterns, Culture Change, Sociability and Navajo Adolescents." *Addictive Diseases.* 1, no. 10 (1974): 97-116.

Much on male and female differences in drinking patterns in this standard descriptive article on Indian drinking.

604. Tucker, Norman. "Nancy Ward, Ghigau of the Cherokees." *Georgia Historical Quarterly.* 53 (June, 1969): 192-200.

An improvement over the usual folkloric treatment of Ward—a key figure in the economic growth of the tribe before Removal.

605. Udall, Louise, ed. *Me And Mine: The Life Story Of Helen Seka-quaptewa.* Tucson: University of Arizona Press, 1969.

An important book about an important Hopi cultural leader—of interest for its articulation of the interface between Hopi tradition and Christianity.

606. Uhlmann, Julie M.Z. "The Impact of Urbanization on the Fertility Behavior of Papago Indian Women." Dissertation, University of California, 1973.

A dissertation which examines the changed and changing attitudes of Papago women undergoing urbanization and the impact of those changes on their behavior with regard to family planning.

607. Underhill, Ruth, ed. "The Autobiography of a Papago Woman (Maria Chona)." *American Anthropological Association Memoirs.* 46, no.31 (1936).

One of the very best narratives, relatively unintruded upon by its hearer, from a remarkable woman with acute memory and an eye for women's culture.

608. United States Department of Education/National Institute of Education. *Conference On The Educational And Occupational Needs Of American Indian Women, 1976.* Washington, DC: Government Printing Office, 1980.

A multi-author (see individual listings) report from a 1976 Albuquerque conference—Indian educators and professionals discuss problems, issues.

609. Van Kirk, Sylvia. *Many Tender Ties: Women In Fur Trade Society In Western Canada, 1670-1870.* Winnipeg, Manitoba: Watson and Dwyer Publishers, Ltd.,1981.

One of two very fine works on domestic relations and the fur trade (See Brown, 1981)—superb descriptions of cross-cultural relations.

610. ———. "The Role of Women in the Fur Trade Society of the Canadian West." Dissertation, University of London, 1975.

The dissertation precursor to Van Kirk's fine book (1981) on the role of Indian women and Metis families in Canada's fur trade.

611. ———. "Thanadelthur." *The Beaver.* (Spring, 1974): 40-45.

From Van Kirk's major later work (1981) on Indian women and the fur trade—a story of a Chippewa woman captured by the Cree—her life with them in a fur trade center.

612. ———. "Women and the Fur Trade." *The Beaver.* (Winter, 1972): 4-21.

A precursor article to Van Kirk's very fine dissertation and book (1981) on the problems and advantages enjoyed by Native women in their marriages and liaisons with fur trade men.

613. ———. "Women in Between: Indian Women in Fur Trade Society." *Historical Papers.* (1977): 31-46.

A short and fine description of the roles and status of Native women as they figured in the domestic and economic relationships of the fur trade—from a later (1980) and very fine dissertation and book.

614. Van Steen, Marcus. *Pauline Johnson, Her Life And Work*. Toronto: Hodder and Stoughton, 1965.

The authoritative biography of the Mohawk poet, actress, cultural leader—including a large selection of her poetry—places her in the appropriate context of cultural leadership.

615. Vanderburgh, Rosamund M. *I Am Nokomis Too: The Biography Of Verva Patronella Johnson*. Don Mills, Ontario: General Publishing Co., 1977.

The extremely interesting biography of an Ojibwa woman—a modern community leader—from the anthropologist who later wrote *Shaman's Daughter* based on this material.

616. Vogelin, C. F. *The Shawnee Female Deity*. New Haven: Yale University Human Relations Area Files, 1936; rep. 1970.

A rare and interesting explanation of female-centered religious behavior.

617. Voight, Frances. *Sacajawea*. New York: G.P. Putnam's and Son, 1967.

Essentially the same tired biography, written every several years anew.

618. Voth, H. R. "Oraibi Natal Customs." *Field Columbian Museum Anthropology Serial*. 6, no. 2 (1905).

One of the many articles on tribal birth customs, this on Hopi. This one with some description of maternal behavior.

619. Waddell, Jack O. "Cross-Sex Attitudes of Papago Male Heavy Drinkers." *Western Canadian Journal Of Anthropology*. 6 (1976): 249-58.

An article which examines the antagonisms toward women that appear during Papago male drinking, and the suggestion that the critical attention to male drinking behavior may illumine female roles.

620. Wagner, Bill. "Lo, the Poor and Sterilized Indian." *America*. 136 (January 29, 1977): 75.

A summary of the events and issues which led up to Indian protest against unecessary sterilization of women.

621. Wagner, Katherine Jean. "An Examination and Description of Acculturation of Selected American Indian Women in An Urban Area." Dissertation, New York University, 1972.

The title is completely descriptive of this very traditional thesis in which "acculturation" is measured according to Western standards.

622. Waldo, Anna Lee. *Sacajawea*. New York: Avon Books, 1978.

An enormous book about a major subject, much mythologized in the past—this one well worth reading for its human and complex, textured fictional portrait of an interesting person and her life.

623. Walker, Tillie Blackbear (Mandan-Hidatsa). "American Indian Children: Foster Care and Adoptions." In Dpt. of Ed./Nat'l. Inst. of Ed. *Conference On The Educational And Occupational Needs Of American Indian Women, 1976*. Washington, DC: Government Printing Office, 1980: 185-210.

About adoption of children and the effects on children and relatives.

624. Wallace, Edith. "Sexual Status and Role Differences." in Robert Heizer, ed. *Handbook Of North American Indians: California, 8*. Washington, DC: Smithsonian Institution-GPO, 1978.

An unusual article in one of the Smithsonian *Handbook* volumes—this very fine one on sexual status and role among California tribes.

625. Waltrip, Lela and Rufus. *Indian Women*. Rutland, Vermont: David MacKay and Co., 1964.

Highly popularized and useless biographies of the standard famous Native women—no surprises.

626. Walworth, Ellen W. *The Life And Times Of Kateri Tekakwitha, The Lily Of The Mohawks*. Montreal: privately published Ms., 1891.

One of the first major religious apologist works about the Mohawk "saint," much more legend than fact about this elusive figure.

627. Wapiti, Marisa. *Ropes Of Sand: Manuscript Of Just A Little Halfbreed*. Smithers, BC: Tanglewood Press, 1972.

The second part of a bad autobiography, meant for the kind of audience who enjoyed Wild West shows—a vulgar popularization of a persistent theme.

628. ———. *Ashes Of Fire, Manuscript Of Just A Little Halfbreed.* Smithers, BC: Tanglewood Press, 1972.
A bad narrative of the "between-two-worlds" variety, meant totally for a non-educated white audience.

629. Warm Springs Singers. "Songs of the Warm Springs Reservation." LP Recording by Canyon Records, c. 1975.
A superb multi-tribal collection of songs from this Oregon reservation—from the women singers who perform a variety of traditional women's songs.

630. Waterman, T.T. and A. L. Kroeber. "Yurok Marriages." *University Of California Publications In American Archaeology And Ethnology.* 35, no. 1 (1934).
The standard work on a rarely studied subject in kinship—describes matchmaking, behavioral and economic expectations.

631. Watkins, Frances B. "Crafts and Industries of the American Indian Women of California and the Southwest." Dissertation, University of Southern California, 1942.
A standard thesis on traditional arts and crafts, with some attention to technologies and tools.

632. Wauneka, Annie (Navajo). "The Dilemma for Indian Women." *Wassaja.* 4 (September, 1976: 8.
A very brief article in which the Navajo leader equates Indian women's rights with Indian rights.

633. Weist, Katherine M. "Plains Indian Women: An Assessment." In Margot Liberty and W. Raymond Wood. *Anthropology On The Great Plains.* Lincoln: University of Nebraska Press, 1980: 255-71.
A decent article that raises scholarly questions about the state of knowledge on Plains women and suggests research priorities.

634. Wertheimer, Barbara Mayer. *We Were There: The Story Of Working Women In America.* New York: Pantheon Books, 1977.
The preface deals, in a highly insulting and shallow fashion with the economic behavior of Native women.

635. Weslager, C. A. "The Delaware Indians As Women." *Journal Of The Washington Academy Of Science.* 34, no. 12 (1944): 381-88.
An interpretation of the "feminization" of the Delawares who lost battles and were thus viewed as "women" by other tribes—very much about the definitions of sex-role attribution.

636. ———. "Further Light on the Delaware Indians as Women." *Journal Of The Washington Academy Of Science.* 37, no. 9 (1947): 298-304.
More from Weslager on the "feminization" of the Delawares who became "women" because they were not victorious in battle.

637. Westermeyer, J. "Sex-Roles At the Indian-Majority Interface in Minnesota." *International Journal Of Social Psychology.* 24 (September, 1978): 189-94.
An unusual if entirely predictable interpretation of male-female sex roles in Indian-white relations.

638. "What More Can You Take Away?" 35mm filmstrip, Color/Sound, 13 minutes, 1970. Produced by Schloat Productions.
A reservation woman who moved to the city talks about Indian identity and conflict.

639. Wheeler, William F. "Sacajawea." *Continental.* 7 (1910): A predictable, ordinary accounting of the lady's adventures as guide to Lewis and Clark.

640. Whiteman, Henrietta V. (Cheyenne). "Insignificance of Humanity, 'Man Is Tampering With the Moon and Stars.' In Dpt. of Ed./ Nat'l. Inst. of Ed. *Conference On The Educational and Occupational Needs Of American Indian Women, 1976.* Washington, DC: Government Printing Office, 1980: 37-62.
A loose analysis of traditional labor patterns—a call for research.

641. "Why Did Gloria Die?" Videotape, B and W, 25 minutes, c. 1975. Produced by Bill Moyers for NBC.
A moving grim portrayal of the life and death of an urban Chippewa woman who moved to Minneapolis from the reservation— shows the struggle with family, jobs and the city.

642. Williams, Agnes F. (Seneca). "Transition From the Reservation to An Urban Setting and the Changing Roles of American Indian Women." In Dpt. of Ed./Nat'l. Inst. of Ed. *Conference On The*

Educational And Occupational Needs Of American Indian Women, 1976. Washington, DC: GPO, 1980: 251-84.
A historical purview on the effects of change—a call for new research.

643. Willis, Jane. *Geneish: An Indian Girlhood.* Toronto: New Press, 1977.
A first person account of boarding school life—intercultural encounters through the eyes of a young girl.

644. Wilson, Dorothy Clarke. *Bright Eyes, The Story Of Suzette La-Flesche.* New York: McGraw-Hill, 1974.
A too-popular treatment of a very interesting, charismatic leader—interesting accounts of LaFlesche's lectures.

645. Wilson, Gilbert and Edward Goodbird (Hidatsa), transcribers. *Waheenee: An Indian Girl's Story.* St. Paul, Minnesota: Webb Publishing Co., 1927; rep.1971 and 1981.
A personal account by a Hidatsa woman on the frontier—interesting for her story itself, but as well for the transcription and questioning by a Native man—her relative.

646. Wilson, Terry (Osage). "Beyond Squaws, Women of the Osage, 1871-1980." *Prologue: The Journal Of The National Archives.* (1982).
A very fine survey and summary article on the history and changing lives of Osage women, by an historian.

647. Winnie, Lucille Jerry/Sah-gan-de-oh (Potawatomie). *Sah-Gan-De-Oh, The Chief's Daughter.* New York: The Vantage Press, 1968.
A potentially decent story flawed by the troublesome and cliched "between-two-worlds" approach—by a well-educated woman who does not acknowledge some harsh realities of modern life.

648. Witt, Shirley Hill (Akwesasne Mohawk). "The Brave-Hearted Women: The Struggle At Wounded Knee." *Akwesasne Notes.* 8, no.2 (1976): 16-17. An activist's account of the women of the American Indian Movement at Wounded Knee II—an attempt to correct the media exclusion of women—widely reprinted (see Katz, 1977; Women of All Red Nations).

649. ———. "Native Women in the World of Work." In Resource Center on Sex Roles-Sex Education. *Sexual Equity And The Minority Woman.* Washington, DC: GPO, 1979.

Discusses the ambivalence and hardships of Native women in professional life—from survey and interviews. Rep. in Dpt. of Labor, 1979.

650. ———. "Native Women Today: Sexism and the Native American Woman." *Civil Rights Digest.* 6, no.3 (1974): 29-35; reprinted in Evelyn Shapiro, ed. *The Women Say, The Men Say.* New York: Dell, 1979.

An outline of internal and external barriers to Native women's equity.

651. Wittstock, Laura Waterman (Seneca). "Native American Women in the Feminist Milieu." In John Maestas, ed. *Contemporary Native American Address.* Salt Lake City, Utah: Brigham Young University, 1976.

Insists that tribalism, not feminism, is correct route for Native women where some tribes have overt, some covert respect for women's power.

652. ———. "Native American Women: Twilight of A Long Maidenhood." In Beverley Lindsay, ed. *Comparative Perspectives Of Third World Women.* New York: Praeger Publishers, 1979.

Offers an overview of the problems and actions of contemporary Native women in the context of Third World status.

653. Women of All Red Nations (WARN). WARN. Porcupine, SD: We Will Remember Group, 1978.

A modern activist tract demanding honoring of Indian land claims and self determination. (See Witt, 1976; Intl. Indian Treaty Council, 1975).

654. Women's Educational Equity Communications Network. *News And Notes:* Special Issue on Native American Women. (Spring,1980).

A short issue with a collection of miscellany—announcements, bibliography, short articles on current events concerning Native women.

655. Women's National Indian Association. *Sketches Of Delightful Work.* Boston: Women's National Indian Association, 1893.

The reformist's Indian "Bible," mostly on work for the Indian reform movement, but filled with descriptions of the LaFlesche lectures on Indian rights.

656. Wood, B. and Barry T. "The Story of Three Navajo Women." *Integrated Education.* 16, no. 2 (1978): 33-35.

An outline of the educational experiences of three traditional Navajo women and the changes that education wrought on them and their perspectives.

657. Wood, Margaret Ann (Navajo). *Native American Fashion.* New York: Van Nostrand Reinhold, 1981.

A history and "how-to" book for the styles of clothing invented and worn by contemporary Native women—decent reference to traditional styles.

658. Wood, Rosemary (Osage). "Health Problems Facing American Indian Women." In Dpt. of Ed./Nat'l. Inst. of Ed. *Conference On The Educational And Occupational Needs Of American Indian Women, 1976.* Washington, DC: Government Printing Office, 1980.

An essential view of a little-discussed and subject by a nurse-educator.

659. Woodward, Isaiah A. "The Influence of the Bosomworth Family on Anglo-Indian Relations in Colonial Georgia, 1745-1759." *Quarterly Review Of Higher Education Among Negroes.* 16 (1948): 83-89.

One of the very few works on the relations between the Creeks, the British colonists and Mary Musgrove's family through the Rev. Bosomworth.

660. Woodward, Mary Twigg. "Juvenile Delinquency Among Indian Girls." Thesis, University of British Columbia, 1949.

A social welfare thesis on adolescent delinquency—very much from the "law-and-order" perspective so popular in the fifties.

661. Wright, Anne L. "Attitudes Toward Childbearing and Menstruation Among the Navajo." In Margarita Kay, ed. *Anthropology Of Human Birth.* Phildelphia: FA Davis, 1981.

A good ethnographic survey of attitudes toward subjects of revitalized interest to anthropologists.

662. ———. "Cultural Variability in the Experience of Menopause: A Comparison of Navajo and Western Data." Dissertation, University of Arizona, 1980.

The dissertation precursor to Wright's fine published studies (1981, 1982, 1983) on Navajo menopause.

663. ——. "An Ethnography of the Navajo Reproductive Cycle." *American Indian Quarterly; A Special Issue on Navajo Women.* (Spring, 1983).

A good overview of the reproductive cycle for the Navajo—one part of a fine series of works by Wright on Navajo women.

664. ——. "Variation in Navajo Menopause." In Voda, A., M. Dinnerstein and O'Donnell, eds. *Changing Perspectives On Menopause.* Austin: University of Texas Press, 1982.

A fine work on the Navajo menopause, part of a series by Wright.

665. Wyman, L. and F. Bailey. "Navajo Girl's Puberty Rite." *New Mexico Anthropologist.* 6-7, no.1 (1943): 3-12.

One of the many brief and rudimentary studies of kinaalda, the Navajo girl's puberty ceremony.

666. Yazzie, Ethelou (Navajo). "Special Problems of Indian Women in Education." In John Maestas, ed. *Contemporary Native American Address.* Salt Lake City, Utah: Brigham Young University, 1976.

A speech describing some of the opportunities and stumbling blocks for Native women in educational settings.

667. Yellowknee, Clara (Metis). "Challenge Facing Metis Women." Alberta National Women's Conference. *First Report.* Edmonton, Alberta: Alberta National Women's Conference, c.1970: 10.

An outline of the difficulties facing Canadian landless, mixedbloods.

668. "Yoimut's Story, The Last Chunut." In F.F. Latta, ed. *Handbook of The Yokut Indians.* Bakersfield, California: Kern County Musuem, 1949: 223-76.

A nineteenth century woman's tale which includes the grim remembrance of an exterminated people.

669. Young, Lucy (Wailaki). "Out of the Past: A True Indian Story, Told by Lucy Young of Round Valley Indian Reservation to Edith V.A. Murphy." *California Historical Society Quarterly.* 20 (December, 1941): 349-74.

A very valuable tale, somewhat marred by the saccharine tone of the editor.

670. Young, Mary E. "Women, Civilization and the Indian Question." In Mabel E. Deutrich and Virginia C. Purdy, eds. *Clio Was A Woman*. Washington, DC: Howard University Press, 1980: 98-110.

A fine article on federal and missionary attempts to undermine Cherokean society through education and training of the women.

671. Young, Philip. "The Mother of Us All." *Kenyon Review*. 24 (Summer, 1962): 391-415.

An initial and major explanation of the Smith-Pocahontas story and its meaning in American literature and culture—an essential and fine work.

672. Zeigen, Robert S. "The Family in Matrilineal Society: A Functional Comparative Analysis of Five Preliterate Cultures." Dissertation, University of Utah, 1952.

An early comparative study of several North American tribal versions of matriorganization—Maidu, Haida, Hopi.

Date Index

Subject Index